To Roger

With love from Sheila

Christmas 1991.

THE RHINE

James Bentley

THE RHINE

Photography by Charlie Waite

GEORGE
PHILIP

British Library Cataloguing in Publication Data
Bentley, James, *1937 –*
The Rhine.
1. Europe. Rhine River region. Description & travel
I. Title
914.3'404878
ISBN 0-540-01177-0

Text © James Bentley 1988
Photographs © Charlie Waite 1988
Maps © George Philip 1988

First published by George Philip,
59/60 Grosvenor Street, London W1X 9DA

Printed in Italy

Half-title illustration **Father Rhine disporting himself at Mannheim.**

Title-page illustration **Lorchhausen, whose parish church is dedicated to the early medieval English missionary St Boniface, nestles among its vineyards, source of some of the finest wines of the Rheingau.**

Contents

In memory of Jim and
Dorothy Bentley

Opposite **The monastery garden and serene
buildings of Kloster Eberbach, founded in 1116
by Cistercian monks who subsequently became
renowned for the quality of their wines.**

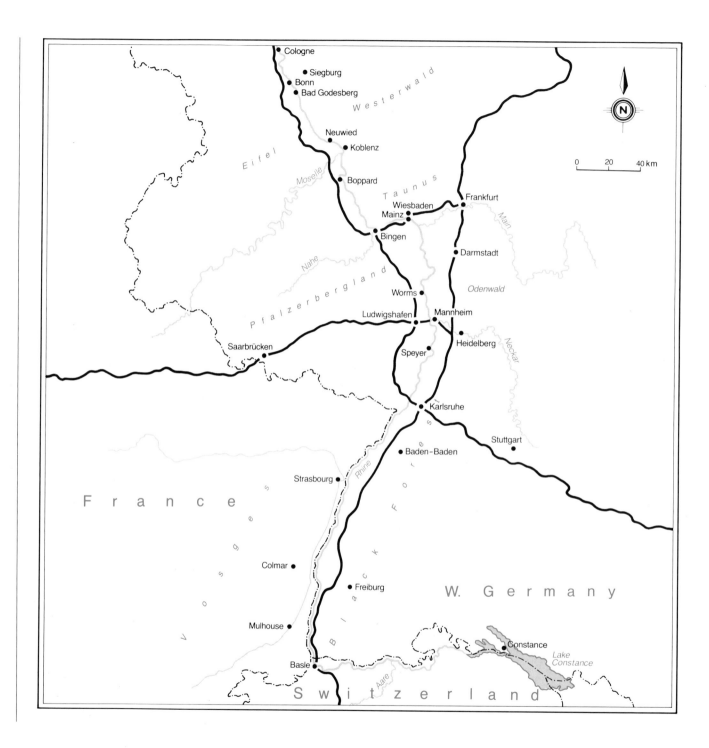

Introduction

On her second trip down the Rhine Mary Shelley, widow of the poet Percy Bysshe Shelley, painted a scene of dreamy romanticism as will sum up the memories of anyone who has made the same journey. 'Memory had painted the Rhine as a scene of enchantment', she wrote, 'and the reality came up to what I remembered. The inferior beauty of the banks of the Moselle enhanced still more the prouder and more romantic glories of the Rhine. The promontories stood in bolder relief – the ruined castles and their ramparts were more extensive and more majestic – the antique spires and gothic abbeys spoke of a princely clergy – and the extent of mouldering walls marked cities belonging to a more powerful population. Each tower-crowned hill – each picturesque ruin – was passed, and gazed upon with eager curiosity and delight. The very names are the titles of volumes of romance; all the spirits of old Germany haunt the place.'

The sources of the Rhine lie high in the Swiss Alps, feeding two foaming mountain streams which join together at Reichenau to form the youthful stage of the great river. From here it flows for 1320 kilometres west and then north across Europe, for much of its length a German river, but acting as a frontier in the south where it divides Switzerland and the Alsace area of France from Germany. Downstream from Cologne, beyond the area covered by this book, it turns west again to empty itself into the North Sea. There is scenery of every kind along its banks, from pastoral rolling countryside to the romantic pine-clad hills of the Black Forest and vine-clad terraces. Sometimes it snakes through deep gorges, with ancient ivy-covered castles perched on either side on their precipitous crags.

This majestic stream, supplemented by its canals and by the waters of the Moselle, the Main and the Neckar, is also a working river, still a major routeway as it has been for centuries. Great barges slide by, sometimes a train of them linked together, sharing the watery road with fishing boats and pleasure craft, flags drooping at their sterns. Often the owner's car is perched bizarrely amidships, beneath washing strung on a line. Sometimes a railway track runs alongside, burrowing into a tunnel where cliffs rise steeply from the water.

The whole region is replete with legends. On the Siebengebirge seven dwarfs took Snow White to their cave. Here Siegfried slew a dragon, fought with Brunhild and was himself slain by the treacherous

Hagen. Vineyards vie in their abundance with the legends of the Rhine. The British used to call Rhine wines 'hock', a name derived from the village of Hockheim, just outside Worms (though some experts argue that it derives instead from Hockheim am Main, just outside Wiesbaden), but this label totally disguised the huge range of wines produced here, including both reds and whites. This flourishing industry was already well established in the Middle Ages, when Catholic monks developed superb varieties of grapes, lovingly cultivated on south-facing slopes. What diverse tastes are insinuated into Rhine wines, as into nearly all the wines of Germany! They graduate in sweet richness through Spätlese and Auslese to Trockenbeerenauslese and Eiswein – the wine created from shrivelled grapes picked after snow has fallen. The same range is produced in Alsace as in Germany across the river, but the wines have different names and a quite distinctive taste. Surprisingly, Alsace not only produces most of the wine drunk in France but is also a centre of beer production, the only one in the country.

The Rhineland has been inhabited for over 500,000 years, if we can believe the conclusions of the archaeologists who dug up the jawbone of *homo erectus* near Heidelberg. Prehistoric Neanderthal man lived in the Rhine valley only 50,000 years ago. His remains are at Bonn. More solid history, so to speak, begins with the Celts, who moved into the region around a thousand years before the birth of Jesus. They gave the great river its name, for Rhine is the Celtic word for current. A Celtic tribe named the Germans occupied the right bank of the river and in 72 BC their king led a

Four of the eight fine varieties of Alsatian wine, displayed by a roadside vendor.

Half-timbered houses reflected in the water of La Petite France, Strasbourg, once the haunt of fishermen and tanners and now treasured for its picturesque balconies, gables and half-timbered houses.

force across the Rhine to conquer the present-day province known as the Palatinate and what is now French Alsace.

By now the Romans were establishing themselves as the most formidable power in the region and by 55 BC Julius Caesar had built the first Rhine bridge, between Andernach and Koblenz. The Roman camp founded by Agrippa in 38 BC is now the great city of Cologne. Faced with continual Celtic uprisings, the Romans built more such camps, and a massive defensive moat and wall, fortified with towers, along the right bank of the river as far as the Taunus mountains and then along the River Main. None the less the native Germans were often a match for the Roman legions. In AD 9, the followers of the redoubtable German Arminius cut three Roman legions to pieces in the Teutoburg forest.

11

The generous earth: corn on the cob drying in the fertile Rhine plain, destined as cattle-feed.

The Romans brought Christianity, but not stability. Soon their barrier was repeatedly overrun, and in one disastrous year, 355, a tribe known as the Alemanni took nearly every ancient Roman city mentioned in this book. Cologne, Mainz, Strasbourg and Speyer all fell. But the supremacy of these Alemanni did not last. First the Burgundians, then the Huns and finally the Franks under the Merovingian King Clovis achieved superiority. Clovis was a Christian, albeit later dubbed a heretic, and he and his successors welcomed British and Irish saints to convert the heathen of these lands.

As Charlemagne's successors made themselves Holy Roman Emperors, so the great cathedral cities steadfastly refused to allow them total sway and local princelings gave other towns precious rights in return for their fealty. In spite of such setbacks as the

Hungarian destruction of Basle in 917, cities prospered and monastic foundations brought a rich culture to the Rhineland, establishing lush vineyards and building magnificent churches. No one ruler managed to dominate the rest, and this new stability enabled the region to flourish. Soon the Rhineland consisted of many principalities, duchies and abbeys, as well as great cities whose archbishops were equal in power to any secular prince. A knight whose *Schloss* commanded the river would charge tolls on the traffic, fixing chains across the water to stop any merchant slipping through without payment. Not surprisingly, the merchants themselves eventually began to provide armed escorts for their vessels.

In the sixteenth century this stability was rudely broken when the Rhineland became the centre of an often violent contest between the followers of Martin Luther's new understanding of Christianity and the traditional Catholic powers. One ominous development was the introduction of foreign mercenaries to put down rival factions. Seizing their chance, the peasants revolted. Whether or not their revolt was partly inspired by Luther's Protestantism, the Reformer himself took care to denounce them, and most of those involved came to a bloody end at the hands of the nobility and their mercenaries. A century later the Thirty Years' War, which began in 1618, brought French, Spanish and Swedish troops into the Rhineland, to do battle with each other and the supporters of the Holy Roman Emperor.

Although the French did best out of this vicious war, it was not well enough for Louis XIV, whose determination to extend his rule into Germany brought fresh brutality. Medieval cities such as

Cobblestones and a cat: the seductive town of Eguisheim, Alsace. Note the curve of the street, a reflection of Eguisheim's curious egg-like shape.

Speyer, Mannheim and Heidelberg scarcely survived the rape of the French soldiery and had to be almost totally rebuilt. By contrast Louis XIV treated Strasbourg and Alsace sparingly, for once tempering his own Catholicism to allow both Protestants and Catholics to worship side by side.

Mercifully this brutality was followed by almost a century of peace which brought with it French civilization, expressed in some of the most exquisite architecture of the Rhineland. Baroque palaces and gardens were created, some used today as entrancing

Above **The quintessential Rhine: a medieval castle rises over Kaub. A profitable toll-station in the Middle Ages, this castle became the headquarters of the Swedish King Gustavus Adolphus during the Thirty Years' War.**

Right **The lion pharmacy at Mainz. This city was the birthplace in *c.* 1400 of Johann Gutenberg, whose invention of movable type revolutionized printing.**

venues for concerts and festivals. The French Revolution and the Napoleonic wars caused more destruction, but not so much as the Rhineland had experienced in the seventeenth century. And the republican ideas brought by Napoleon's armies were welcome to many in German-speaking Rhineland. As Victor Hugo put it in 1838, 'One could say that the right bank of the Rhine belongs as much to Napoleon as to Charlemagne.' But Bonaparte was defeated and much of the Rhineland became Prussian. In 1870 Otto von Bismarck managed to provoke the French Emperor Napoleon III into war. The French lost and Germany took over Alsace. It was Bismarck who was also responsible for the unification of Germany, the first time this heterogeneous collection of states was welded into a single entity. In the eighteenth century, for instance, more than 300 rulers dominated their own little patch of the country, the quaint titles they adopted – landgrave, elector, elector palatine, prince-elector and so on – a continuing theme throughout this book.

With the defeat of Germany and its allies in World War I, the French re-occupied the Rhineland with a vengeance, provoking a backlash which Adolf Hitler was able to exploit when his armies marched in in 1936. World War II also saw Alsace once again in German hands, to be returned to France only with the defeat of Nazi Germany and after the sad destruction of many fine buildings and works of art. Since then most of the towns and cities along the great river have been sumptuously restored and the legacies of the Rhine's more distant turbulent past have become key features of its romantic appeal. Without the uncertainties of the Middle Ages, we would not now enjoy ancient castles overlooking the crags of the river, and a galaxy of

Rhens is full of delightful corners such as this.

Dormer windows in Koblenz, a city almost completely destroyed in World War II and beautifully restored.

lovely fortified villages and towns, whose powerful churches and often half-ruined bastions have miraculously survived to this day.

The Rhineland, like the Rhine itself, has many facets. Countless novelists and poets have attempted to encapsulate the charms of this exquisite region of Europe through which flows what Thomas Carlyle declared to be the 'beautifullest river on earth'. I have not seen every river on earth, but I think Victor Hugo was right when he said that the Rhine has every quality a river needs: sometimes wide, sometimes narrow; at times limpid, at other times an impenetrable bluey-green; then a torrent pouring into an abyss; soon a smoothly flowing stream and next as wide as a lake; and always a noble river rejoicing in its strength.

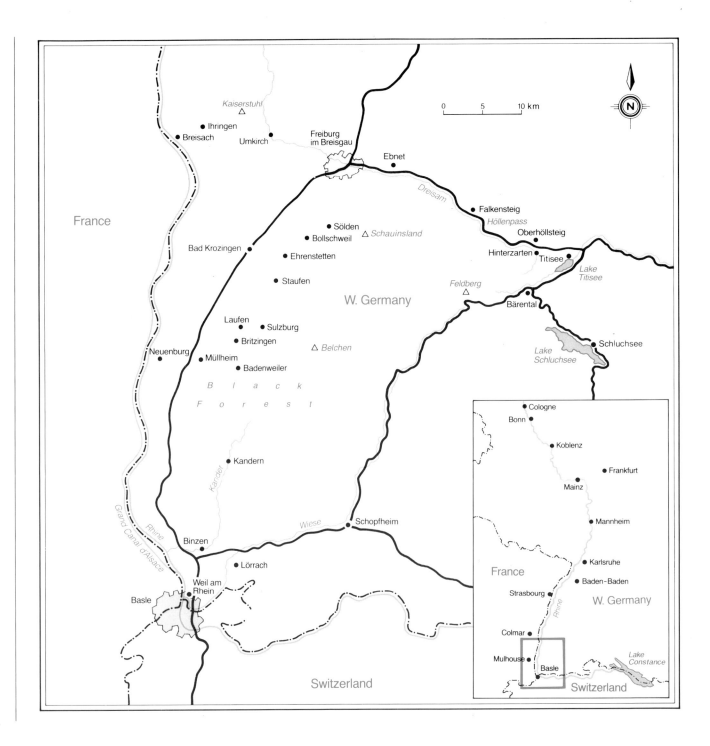

1
In the Black Forest

Basle – Kandern – Badenweiler – Staufen –
Freiburg – Titisee – Schluchsee – Breisach –
Bad Krozingen – Müllheim

One of the delights of the upper Rhine is that it is bordered to the east by the exquisite and sometimes awe-inspiring hills of the Schwarzwald, or Black Forest, and to the west by the vine-covered slopes of Alsace. The motorway which runs from Weil am Rhein at the Swiss border to Freiburg im Breisgau is enhanced beyond the dreams of most motorway drivers by skirting the great river itself for much of its course. Still more enchanting is the old *Landstrasse* to Freiburg, wandering through the lower slopes of the Black Forest and continually emerging from the mysterious green woods for another glimpse of the river.

The villages through which this *Landstrasse* passes are part of the Baden wine road. Once most of the wines drunk in the rest of Germany were produced here, but its supremacy was destroyed first by phylloxera, which ruined its vineyards in the 1870s, and then by a disastrous policy of replanting inferior vines. Happily these have now been replaced by the finest stock. Today nearly eighty per cent of the wines of Baden are white, largely produced from the Müller-Thurgau grape with smaller quantities of Riesling, Gutedel, Ruländer and other varieties. All these and the rich red Spätburgunder can be sampled in the wine *Stuben* which feature in every village.

Valleys and peaks, woodlands and lush green meadows characterize this part of the Black Forest, and cool lakes have filled some of the low-lying regions. This is a land of smallholdings, studded with the uniquely picturesque *Schwarzwaldhäuser*, with their eaves projecting out on either side like wings. Often the gable ends shelter a narrow porch on the first floor, a relic of the not too distant times when cattle and chickens were housed on the ground floor. Indeed, on some of the remoter farms animals and humans still live under the same roof. When Mark Twain visited the Black Forest in 1880 he spotted one inevitable consequence of this pattern of life: huge piles of manure outside each farmhouse. 'We became very familiar with the fertiliser of the Forest', he wrote, and he and his companions fell unconsciously into the habit of judging a farmer's station in life by this outward and eloquent sign. 'Sometimes we said, ''Here is a poor devil, this is manifest.'' When we saw a stately accumulation, we said, ''Here is a banker.'' When we encountered a country seat surrounded by an Alpine pomp of manure, we said, ''Doubtless a duke lives here.'' '

Today such piles of manure are rare, as the farmers now live as much off timber as cattle. The forests that once blanketed the mountain slopes are now felled in broad swathes, the peace of the valleys disturbed by chain-saws and tractor engines. Thousands of trees are floated down the Rhine as far as Holland, bound together in huge rafts 300 metres long. Tourists first started to come here in the eighteenth century, and soon the hospitable climate of this part of Germany became renowned. For much of the year you can sit out of doors in the evening, sipping wine and watching the shadows darkening on the hills or the lights of boats on the Rhine; yet the peaks will often be snow-covered, and this is a region where skiing has become a profitable tourist industry. Many Black Forest farmers augment their income by catering to the holiday trade.

The great river which divides France from Germany rises many miles further south in the Swiss Alps. From here it flows north in a deeply cleft valley, passing little Liechtenstein on its journey to Lake Constance. At the western end of the lake, where the Rhine becomes a river again, the waters celebrate their new found freedom in the thundering Schaffhausen falls, the most impressive in Europe. 'What words can express – for indeed, for many ideas and emotions there are no words – the feeling excited by the tumult,

the uproar and matchless beauty of a cataract, with its eternal, ever-changing veil of misty spray,' exclaimed Mary Shelley, inspired by the power and beauty of the water. At Basle to the west the river turns north, leaving the Alps behind.

Basle is the second largest town in Switzerland, its population of 200,000 swelled by about a million visitors at the time of its annual trade fair. Situated where the borders of France, Germany and Switzerland meet, Basle stands at a major European crossroads and not surprisingly generates a good third of Switzerland's customs revenues. As Switzerland's only port, opened in 1924, it thrives off the river trade, and there are three railway stations here, one Swiss, one French and one German. The affluence so obvious in its streets is based on a wide range of industries: engineering and textiles, chemicals and pharmaceuticals. In theory, Basle ought to have been spoiled, transformed by commercial and industrial success into a modern town, leaving behind the one that so enchanted Gerard Manley Hopkins when he came here in 1868. 'Nothing could be more taking and fantastic', he wrote excitedly to a friend. In fact it remains as enticing as ever.

Basle divides into two parts, Greater Basle (Grossebasel) climbing up the steep left bank of the Rhine, and Little Basle (Kleinbasel) situated on the right bank. When Gerard Manley Hopkins visited the town, the ancient bridge which had linked the two since 1226 still survived, although its wooden supports had long been replaced in stone. Standing

Gästehaus
Roter Ochse

Right **Water and snow in the Black Forest, where once remote villages are now centres for winter sports.**

Left **A painted sign on the wall of an inn high above the Rhine reflects the particular attractions of this succulent region of Germany.**

Solid prosperity: a house in Ritterstrasse, Basle, displays the substantial fortune of a Swiss merchant.

looking at the powerful river, the poet felt it shake beneath him.

Basle is washed not just by the Rhine but by two other rivers as well, although the Rhine is incomparably the greatest of the three, already 265 metres wide at this point. One Easter I stayed in nearby Lörrach, just over the German border, with the mother of a former au-pair girl who had shared my English home. Frau Zerzau followed the delightful German custom of decorating hard-boiled eggs with brightly coloured patterns to mark the day of Our Lord's resurrection and I took some in a bag up to Basle cathedral and sat there on a wall to eat them.

From here I could see the ancient bastion 20 metres above the river known as the *Pfalz*, where Hopkins had walked over a century earlier. The trees he saw are still there, as well as one of the fountains he admired very much, placed here in 1784. Below me the bank fell so steeply away that I could have dropped the eggshells straight down into the water. From the *Pfalz* you can see far across the river, to the hills of the Black Forest, west to the Jura mountains and (on a clear day) even to the Vosges.

The red sandstone spires of Basle cathedral rise 65 metres from its west end, picturesquely crocketed at the top. St George's spire on the left was finished in 1472, St Martin's on the right in 1500, each identified by equestrian carvings of their respective saints set at the foot of the towers. George rides as a knight, slaying the dragon; Martin is a Roman centurion, handing over half his cloak to a beggar. Their horses have superb manes. As your eyes descend the rest of the cathedral's west front it seems sterner, until you reach the two gothic portals. That on the west is sculpted with statues of the Holy Roman Emperor Heinrich II and his wife Kunigunde, and of the unlikely figures of a foolish virgin led astray by her seducer.

Heinrich II is here because he built Basle cathedral in the second decade of the eleventh century, on the site of an earlier building founded by Charlemagne. Heinrich's cathedral had to be restored in 1185 after a fire, and then largely rebuilt when it was virtually destroyed by an earthquake in 1356. The new work was in the fashionable gothic style. Severely damaged again in 1529, the building we see today was thoroughly restored in the nineteenth century.

Oddly enough, when Victor Hugo visited Basle in the mid nineteenth century the cathedral initially shocked him and then filled him with anger. He lamented the lack of old stained-glass windows and he considered the stone indecently red for such a noble building. He soon changed his mind, bewitched by the romantic spires and the coloured roof tiles. The sculpted women on the façade enchanted him the way most women fascinated Victor Hugo. Visitors to Basle cathedral fall under the same spell today, even those

British whose experience of sandstone minsters may well be limited to the rather insipid example at Coventry.

What was saved from the twelfth-century cathedral is beautiful. Walk round to the north transept to see the St Gallus portal, six slender pillars – two plain, two double and two twisted – supporting three unadorned round arches. Nothing could be less pretentious. The whole is then enriched by carvings of St Peter, St Paul and the wise and foolish virgins. Above this delicate survival now eight centuries old a powerful romanesque rose window depicts the wheel of fortune. Walk on into the old cathedral cloisters, as always the last resting-place of men who were once considered great but now lie forgotten.

The most illustrious lying here is the Protestant

As the English architect G. E. Street wrote in 1855, 'There are few things in the world so fine as a mighty river, few rivers so fine as the Rhine, and few spots so favourable for its contemplation as the balcony at Basle.'

Reformer Johannes Hussgen, the man who called himself Oecolampadius and whose bones remind us that Basle cathedral is no longer a Catholic church but a Protestant minster. Oecolampadius was appointed cathedral preacher in 1515, at a time when the first waves of the Reformation were dividing Europe. For a time his adherence to the doctrines of the Reformers wavered. First he supported Martin Luther, but in 1520 Oecolampadius abandoned Luther's teaching and

became a Catholic monk. Two years later he was back in Basle, his vows renounced and his commitment to the Reformation firm. By 1528 the former priest and monk had found himself a wife. Such was his influence that soon the Canton of Berne went over to the Reformation, perhaps because Johannes Oecolampadius was never an extremist. The doctrinal statement which he drafted is a model of moderation. Adopted by the town council after his death it is known as the Confession of Basle, and committed moderation remains the tone of Basle Protestants to this day. The huge wine flagons on display in the exhibition of communion plate housed in the minster are evocative reminders of one consequence of the Reformation. As soon as the Reformers decided that everyone (not just the priest) should receive wine as well as bread at the Christian altar, a good deal more wine was needed for every celebration.

When the essayist Michel de Montaigne visited Basle in 1580 he was fascinated to see a remarkable spirit of religious toleration developing. He met many learned men, and judged that they were not in agreement over their religion, 'some calling themselves Zwinglians', as he noted, 'others Calvinists and others Martinists' (by which he meant followers of Martin Luther). 'He was informed', wrote his secretary, 'that many still fostered the Roman Catholic religion in their hearts.' In consequence Basle did not see the kind of mindless destruction which characterized followers of the new beliefs elsewhere. Images in stained-glass windows were not poked out as being sacrilegious. Most people still received the bread of Holy Communion in their mouths, according to the Catholic fashion; 'however', as Montaigne and his secretary

The shady gothic cloisters of Basle cathedral, the burial ground of scholarly theologians of the Middle Ages and passionate advocates of the Reformation.

observed, 'anyone who wants may put out his hand for it' – the Protestant custom – 'and the ministers do not dare to touch this chord in these differences in religion.' One fascinating anomaly the Frenchmen observed was that the citizens still paid the Catholic bishop an excellent annual income of 50,000 livres and continued to follow their ancient custom of electing a new bishop when the see fell vacant, although the bishop himself was extremely hostile to the Protestants of Basle and had taken up residence outside the city.

Such toleration can be partly explained by the fact that Basle's culture and the theological faculty of its great university attracted devout men of diverse religious faith during the upheavals of the Reformation. As well as Oecolampadius, the Reformer Ulrich Zwingli studied here from 1502 to 1506, returning to discuss theology with Erasmus of Rotterdam when he began to teach humanism at the university. Erasmus had harsh words for his fellow Catholics, but he disliked Protestantism more and left the city for Freiburg in 1529. Seven years later he died on a visit to Basle, which is why his bones rest in the cathedral. As for John Calvin, his seminal *Institutes of the Christian Religion* was both written and published here.

In fact Basle's tolerant ways soon began to work to the city's own profit. Persecuted Huguenots fled here from France after the revocation of the Edict of Nantes in 1685, bringing their skill at weaving silk with them. Other religious refugees from Catholic Italy and Holland brought a taste of alien cultures and new talent and trade contacts with the outside world. Basle's prosperity was enhanced at the end of the Thirty Years' War, when the greatest of all her mayors, Johann Rudolf Wettstein, managed to persuade all the great powers to respect the city's freedom and allow her to live in peace.

The interior of Basle minster, where the mild and brilliant Erasmus lies and where Zwingli preached, is vast and impressive, with an organ supported on a balcony of 1381 and a richly carved stone pulpit dating from a hundred years later. The carvings on the delightful eight-sided font show Jesus's baptism, as one might expect, but also St Lawrence with the gridiron on which he was roasted and St James, the patron saint of pilgrims. In case you do not recognize James from the pilgrim's cockleshell on his hat, he carries another on his shirt.

Although Erasmus was buried here, his body was later exhumed and only brought back again in 1928. I found his gravestone at the east end of the north aisle with difficulty and failed to translate his lengthy Latin epitaph. Feeling defeated, I scurried from the cathedral and took Augustinergasse past a fourteenth-century fountain and the museum of natural and local history. Huge frescoes painted by Arnold Böcklin in the 1860s decorate the staircase of this classical building, appropriately depicting scenes from Greek mythology. I have never managed to get past them into the museum itself, preferring to stroll on along the Rheinsprung to gaze at two extremely pretty buildings: the White House, built in the 1760s, and the fourteenth-century Blue House.

Basle's university library is also here. In Michel de Montaigne's time the medical school of Basle university was as renowned as its theological faculty. A surgeon named Oswald Baer carried out the first ever public dissection of a corpse here and the oldest existing example of a human skeleton prepared for display – still to be seen in the city anatomical collection – was the work of a brilliant physician from Brussels called Andreas Versalis, who came to Basle in 1542. Montaigne was greatly attracted by Basle's intellectuals and their 'handsome public library on the river', although his journal records his distaste when he watched 'a poor man's little boy cut open for rupture and treated very roughly by the surgeon'.

Montaigne also complained about the unclean bed linen in Swiss hotels – a fault long since remedied. Two and a half centuries later Charles Dickens described Switzerland in *The Uncommercial Traveller* as a country of 'wooden houses, innocent cakes, thin butter soup, and spotless little inn bedrooms with a family likeness to Dairies'. His reservations concerned the Swiss love of hunting: wherever he went outside the villages and towns bullets whizzed by dangerously close. For my part I have to say that I have never found dirty linen in Basle bedrooms nor been shot at when driving back to Germany or France.

Turn left from the Rheinsprung up Archivegässlein to see one of the finest fountains in Basle, topped by a halbardier and created by Hans Tobell in 1547. To the right stands St Martin's church, rebuilt like the cathedral after the earthquake of 1356 and now only used for concerts. In consequence the church is excellently preserved (and always warm inside), its memorials and ornamented tombstones neat and tidy around the walls. Returning to the Rheinsprung and continuing downhill to the Rhine, you pass houses of all ages and designs. Happily most have their dates inscribed on the walls, and sometimes they are named: a house of 1719; the house of Hans Duttelbach, the house of the town crier, dated 1573; the *Walpurgisnacht* house, dated 1438; the house of the wild man, dated 1443; and so on.

The Rheinsprung reaches the Rhine at the point where Hopkins crossed the ancient wooden bridge and felt it shudder. Alas, this structure was replaced in 1905 by the present Mittlere Brücke, none the less a splendid enough construction with five arches. A little turret from the old bridge – in fact a chapel built in 1478 – is set half-way along. On the south side is Carl Burckhardt's majestic bronze statue of an Amazon leading her horse, created in 1926.

Not far from here, left along Eisengasse, is Basle's market square, dominated by the stupendous,

---

The delicious clock on Basle town hall, a late medieval fancy obviously created by clockmakers with a sense of fun.

RENOVATUM ET AMPLI
FICATUM ANNO DOMINI
MDCCCCI

romantically asymmetrical pink town hall, from whose open-air pulpit preachers would harangue the citizens. It was built in the first decade of the sixteenth century, and when the building was restored at the end of the nineteenth the architect in charge had the excellent idea of adding a tower. I find every diverse element enchanting – the early sixteenth-century frescoes by Hans Bock, the double-storeyed oriel window, the fairy-tale clock guarded by a king, two queens and a fiery knight surmounted by the banner of Basle, and the slender golden spire. The dormer window carries the head of a green man, leaves growing from his mouth.

Go inside the courtyard, dominated by the statue of another fearsome soldier, the bearded Munatius Planeus, the Roman general who established a colony near here on the banks of the Rhine in 27 BC. Placed here in 1580, he is dressed in a Roman tunic, with gold braid and red underwear. As you enter the courtyard the walls to left and right are decorated with seventeenth-century wall-paintings by Hans Bock the Elder and his son. The courtyard itself is charmingly frescoed with cherubs, a noble procession, minstrels, dogs and a representation of Diana the Huntress. Mermaids peer from the roundels. Here too are some examples of those complacent mottoes which rich merchants have always used to conceal their business acumen under a cloak of piety: 'Freedom is better than silver and gold'; 'Whoever does good will receive good in return'; 'Where there is unity, there is God's reward'. Only the Swiss could get away with such pompous sentiments, for they have remained prosperous, free, sober, godly (till recently) and united, in spite of every difference of religion, language and tradition in their cantons.

Before leaving the courtyard, go through the ornamental gateway of 1547 and climb the arcaded

---

A frescoed wall in Basle's flamboyant town hall.

Some of the riotous renaissance decoration which enhances Basle town hall, with beautifully carved birds pecking away at the grapes on the vines.

---

steps with carvings of a wild boar and a monkey peering down from the vaults above. You will be rewarded with a view of the remains of Basle's huge city fortifications. Of the three surviving gates of this town, the fifteenth-century Spalantor (St Paul's gate) is one of the most remarkable in Europe. Today Basle's green and yellow tramcars run in and out of it.

Many other fine buildings ring the market square, such as the renaissance Geltzenzunfthaus built in 1578 by the wine merchants of Basle, or the Schlüsselzunft built for the key-makers' guild. Here too are splendid art nouveau buildings now housing famous shops: Zoller's bakery; Haegeli's cigarette corner; the Confiserie Schiesser. Window-shoppers can wander down

The enjoyment of Black Forest wine is by no means only confined to monks.

the pedestrianized Freie Strasse from the square, lined with shoeshops, jewellers, dress-shops, tailors, furriers and bookshops. Another lovely square close by houses the fish market, with its enchanting fifteenth-century fountain supporting statues of the Virgin Mary, St Peter and St Paul.

In the market square itself, every day except Sunday, colourful umbrellas like giant mushrooms shelter stalls piled high with fruit, flowers and vegetables, and twice a month a flea-market is also held here. The square contains one of those ubiquitous Swiss restaurants known as Mövenpick, where the food is always serviceable. I prefer to patronize one of the many wine bars selling a wide variety of German, French and Italian vintages. Both wine and food are invariably more expensive than you expect here. As a

bonus, Mövenpick's circular downstairs bar even serves non-alcoholic beers.

But you do not need to eat expensively in Basle. Away from the centre you can find veal and liver dishes at reasonable prices. Sometimes, though, it is worth paying more. I was directed to a restaurant serving the celebrated Basle *Herrenschnitzel*, a veal cutlet cooked in breadcrumbs and stuffed with goose liver as well as cheese. I liked it so much that I visited the restaurant (the Schützenhaus) to try the dish a second time.

Fish restaurants abound in Basle, though nowadays they derive their fish not from the polluted Rhine but from the River Aare. There are also many establishments with names such as Ceresio and Chez Donati, reminding you that you can also eat gnocchi and lasagne here, prepared by Swiss chefs whose origins are Italian. One of the most mixed-up meals I had was at Basle central station, where I followed French onion soup with Alsatian sauerkraut, both prepared by Swiss chefs.

Steps lead from the fish market up the Kellergässlein, past a strange-looking naked lady painted on the wall in 1910 by Alfred Pellegrini (who was born in 1881). She is supposed to depict someone who has been ill and is now recovering. In the square half-way up the steps is an equally odd-looking boy, sculpted in 1981, the work of Willy Hege (who was born in 1907). Both artists were commissioned by the city authorities – a fine tradition of municipal support for the arts, whatever you think of the results.

At the top of the steps stands the late gothic church of St Peter, finished in the fourteenth century, its lovely nave windows stained and fired a century later. From the style of its case I think that the eighteenth-century organ is by one of the great Silbermann brothers, although the front pipes are newer. To the right is a faded but still delightful fifteenth-century fresco of the entombment of Jesus. Here his dead body is being placed in a stone coffin, not in the sepulchre with a boulder placed against it as described in the Bible. Every fragment of fresco in this church is worth seeking out.

In the church square stands a bust of the poet Johann Peter Hebel, a literary oddity if ever there was one. Hebel's father died when he was scarcely a year old. Brought up in utter poverty in the Wiese valley, he became a brilliant scholar, was soon recognized as such and educated at the university of Erlangen. His chosen subject was theology. Soon he was director of the grammar school at Karlsruhe. But what made him famous were his popular narrative poems written in the local dialect. 'The whole world', said Goethe, 'is turned into a bucolic idyll by Hebel.' Hebel had the gift of appealing to sentimental Protestant religiosity. Thus his poem *Sunday Morning* imagines that even the cock will not crow on the day the church decrees that no one shall work:

> Gently on tiptoe Sunday creeps,
> Cheerfully from the stars he peeps,
> Mortals all asleep below,
> None in the village hears him go;
> Even chanticleer keeps very still,
> For Sunday whispered, 'twas his will.'

Hebel died near Heidelberg in 1826. His bust outside St Peter's looks out over the municipal park and the rich botanical garden, but he cannot quite see the former church of the Dominicans to the right down Petersgraben. A pity, for this fine building, consecrated in 1261, has a gothic belfry dating from 1523 and another Silbermann organ. If you have time it is well worth trying to get inside, especially for one of the many concerts given here. I have heard Bach played on the organ, though to my ear the tone was much louder and harsher than what you would usually expect from the Silbermann family. The organ-case, however, is perfect.

The Dominican church brings me back to the Rhine, and to a square once famous for a celebrated dance of death, painted on the wall of the church graveyard in 1440 and smashed by Napoleon's troops in 1805. The graveyard north of the church no longer exists and now a comical modern statue of Janus by Otto Bäuminger stands here, showing him twisted and looking both ways. Across the road at no. 2 Totentanz-platz Johann Peter Hebel was born on 10 May 1760.

If you turn right here along the left bank of the Rhine you reach the restaurant of the Magi (Drei Könige am Rhein), which is said to be the oldest in Switzerland. Here you can sit on a terrace overlooking the river, eating veal and beef in the Swiss style, or French guinea fowl. Continue walking along the river bank and you once again reach the Mittlere Brücke.

Basle of course offers many more treats than those covered in this short tour. Its former Franciscan church (the Barfüsserkirche), built in the fourteenth century, is today the splendid home of the town's history museum. Another refuge on wet afternoons is the gallery of fine arts, where the attractions of works by Hans Holbein the Younger vie with a fine collection of Cubist paintings, including important canvases by Picasso, Braque and Gris. When the town council bought Picasso's touching *Seated Harlequin* and his *Two Brothers* in 1967, the artist was so pleased that he presented the gallery with four other works. It also features many pictures by the Dada and surrealist artist Hans Arp, who was born in Basle in 1887.

Take an hour or two to wander through the zoological garden (which the Baslers dub the 'Zolli'), one of the oldest in Europe. Completely reorganized in 1949, it now cares for some 2500 animals, including species rare in Swiss zoos, such as the black panther and the threatened okapi. If you prefer books to animals, visit the university library, rich in humanist works by Erasmus and by Protestants of the calibre of Zwingli and Philip Melanchthon. Ironically, this university, the first in all Switzerland and now an intellectual fount of Protestant history, was founded in 1460 by Pope Pius II, who had visited Basle for an abortive ecumenical council which utterly failed to solve the problems caused for the Church by reforming zealots and anti-papal Catholics.

If you have time cross into Little Basle, a completely different town, its buildings chiefly fronted with nineteenth-century façades and its shops cheaper than in Greater Basle. Kleinbasel is also the haunt of dealers in second-hand goods and antiques, as well as the site of the trade fairs. Both the March antiques fair and the June art fair proved simultaneously fascinating and far beyond the reaches of my pocket. Kleinbasel also seems to be favoured by Basle's nightclubs, including one I saw in Clarastrasse offering a 'family show' at weekends. Since I didn't have my family with me, I didn't see the show.

Leave Basle by the motorway which is signposted *Deutschland* and the city of Karlsruhe, crossing over the Rhine at Weil. This is where the river swings north, flowing for some 300 kilometres along the so-called *Graben*, a wide and fertile rift valley. The scenery on both sides of the river is magnificent. To the left is Alsace, a land of orchards and vineyards, of hops and half-timbered houses, a land fought over by Germans and French for centuries and now French – though its people remain almost as fiercely independent as the Basques – and their ways, architecture, charm and gastronomy are unique to themselves. In the distance rise the Vosges mountains, their lower slopes covered in vineyards.

Weil am Rhein, 3 kilometres from Basle, lies at a spot where Switzerland, Germany and France meet, and has been an important crossing-point since monks from St Gallen founded the town in the eighth century. Take the first exit off the motorway and follow the road to Kandern through Binzen, bearing left out of the village along the lovely Kander valley.

Kandern's former town hall was built in the fifteenth century and is but one delight of this pretty white and yellow town, which enjoyed a burst of architectural expansion in the next 200 years. Old mills (the Fischermühle dates from 1452), a hunting-lodge of 1589, shady courtyards and fountains add to its charm, and the Protestant church, built by Friedrich Weinbrenner of Karlsruhe in the 1820s, by no means spoils it. Kandern has two specialities: ceramics and its own pretzel (Kandern *Brezel*). The local museum introduced me to a potter I had never heard of, Max Laueger, whose art nouveau creations are unpretentiously lovely – he died aged 88 in 1952 – and to my surprise I discovered that the celebrated Expressionist painter August Macke had made his home here. And no less a poet than Johann Peter Hebel sang in praise of the local wine:

> *Jetzt schwingen wir den Hut,*
> *Der Wein, der war so gut.*

which I roughly translate as:

> Let everyone raise a hat
> To wine as good as that.

The wine goes well with Kandern pretzels, which you can eat sitting in the square outside the white-walled inn with green shutters, gently lulled by the sound of the fountain.

For those who want to explore the Black Forest, or go riding in the hills, this would be an excellent place to stay. The road to Badenweiler wends its way through breathtakingly beautiful wooded hills with small villages nestling by streams and in sheltered hollows. In spring and early summer the meadows are filled with a kaleidoscope of wild flowers – blue, mauve, pink, yellow, white and red – some of them wild orchids.

After 2 kilometres a short detour to the right leads

The tracery of branches against a winter sky is one of the pleasures of the fringes of the Black Forest.

up a thickly wooded road to Schloss Bürgeln, once the property of the lords of Kaltenbach. Burnt down, it was rebuilt in the rococo style in 1762. It is well worth panting up the steep path from the car park for the sudden view of the *Schloss* perched above the trees as delicately as a China teapot on a green table-cloth. After the climb take refreshment in the *Schloss* restaurant before exploring its painted and stuccoed rooms and its fine chapel. The fragile lacy ironwork of the balcony and railings outside the castle matches the delicacy of the stucco-work inside.

From the castle's hilltop site there are superb views of the Rhine valley and the Vosges mountains across the river in Alsace-Lorraine. Panoramas continue to unfold as you follow the picturesque (and hair-raisingly narrow) road east from here into Baden-weiler, some 12 kilometres from Kandern. A network of vineyards appears on your right, and then the huge plain in which the town is set stretches before you. Set some 426 metres above sea-level, Badenweiler has been a spa since the Romans came here to enjoy the hot springs in the first century AD. I have never tried the waters of the modern spa, but can testify that the Margrafenbad of 1972 is splendidly situated in a subtropical park warmed by the springs and covering 16 hectares. An indoor pool is covered by an impressive glasshouse, and the climate is often suitable for swimming in the adjoining outdoor pool. The Margrafenbad offers all sorts of bizarrely named treatments – not just the familiar Kneipp water cure invented by a German clergyman at the beginning of the last century, but also 'inhalation', something called the Fango, 'carbonic acid baths', private thermal baths and an indoor hot bath for underwater exercise. I preferred to sit on the sun terrace and watch the patients (if that is the right word) walk down to the rest-lawn after treating their lumbago, arthritis, muscular troubles, heart complaints and circulation problems (for the thermal springs at Badenweiler claim to ease all these). Not surprisingly, many hotels have

set up a profitable trade in doing good here, and many of them have their own curative treatments.

Like all such spas, Badenweiler hosts concerts, with open-air performances on the bandstand in the park. Here there is room for a string band of about a dozen musicians, who play Strauss and Rossini amongst enormous floral displays. The old Roman baths, discovered in 1784, can now be visited and there are art treasures to be viewed in the mid sixteenth-century grand-ducal palace. Or simply stroll through the lovely square at the centre of the town with its shady plane trees and its fountain. A little stream ripples through the streets, past sturdy houses characteristically painted in strong colours. At night everything is gaily illuminated, and the ruined old *Schloss*, dramatically lit, beams benignly down.

A few kilometres further north lies Britzingen, reached along a road which passes a massive clinic on the right. It is difficult not to be moved by the sight of so many crippled people who have come or been brought here in the hope of a cure. We are now into vineyard country, the serried ranks of the vines marching relentlessly away on either side. Notice the way in which they have been tied to their stakes or wires, and how they do things differently on the other side of the Rhine.

Soon the wine road runs through the little village of Laufen, famed in these parts for its flower-gardens, and here turns right to visit the scarcely larger town of Sulzburg, with its white and pink medieval gate. When I was there this ancient monument was still inhabited, with curtains at the three windows over the round arch. The first church you come across in Sulzburg has been turned into a museum of regional buildings, but much more interesting is the church of St Cyriak, reached by following the signs which take you past a lime tree 4 metres in circumference, said to be 250 years old.

Cyriacus was a Roman Christian at a time when his faith was outlawed. Arrested by the authorities for

trying to help some of his fellow-Christians who were already imprisoned, he gained favour by curing the Emperor Diocletian's daughter of possession. The grateful Diocletian gave him a house, which Cyriacus turned into a church. He then went to Persia, found to his delight that the King of Persia's daughter was also possessed, and cured her. But when he returned to Rome Diocletian was dead, and his successor Maximian had a fanatical hatred of Christianity; in 309 he had Cyriacus beheaded.

Why monks should have founded a church at Sulzburg in the year 993 in honour of a martyr who died in 309 I cannot say; but Cyriacus has inspired the creation of a beautiful romanesque house of God. The stunningly simple exterior with its low, round apse conceals a cool three-aisled basilica supported on square pillars and round arches, airy and light. Over the entrance is a romanesque carving of a haloed Jesus, the founders of the church kneeling at his feet.

The main road continues from here to Staufen. Its *Schloss* looms ahead, standing powerfully above the modern town. Make your way to the medieval quarter at its heart, where the town hall in the main square is covered with coats of arms and dated 1546. Not far away is the Gasthof zum Löwen, built in 1407. It was here Dr Johann Faust finally paid his debt to the devil in 1539 and was hauled off to Hell, commemorated in a picture on the wall of Satan claiming his prey. The house dated 1756 opposite is in fact built around a medieval courtyard. In warm weather awnings and parasols provide welcome shade outside the cafés in the square, and there are flowers everywhere, even decking the little fountain in the centre.

Strolling along the picturesque main street, with streams running on either side, you turn a corner to get an unexpected view of vineyards rising up to the ruined *Schloss*, built by the lords of Staufen in the twelfth century. The hill on which it stands is said to resemble an upturned chalice – a *Stouf* in early German, hence the name Staufen. It is well worth

Statues of Freiburg's imperial protectors guard the city's market hall of 1520.

climbing up to the ruined castle to take yourself back in time and for one of the finest views of Mount Belchen, the most impressive of all the peaks in the Black Forest. Back in Staufen again you could sample a slice of Black Forest gâteau or one of the town's famous liqueurs.

Freiburg im Breisgau is now only 18 kilometres away. Carry on along the wine road through Ehrenstetten and Bollschweil, and then look for the turning right which leads through exquisite country-side to the baroque monastery buildings which Peter Thumb designed for the Cluniacs of the convent of St Ulrich in 1740. Another treasure along the Freiburg road is the fine seventeenth-century church at Sölden, all that remains of a monastery destroyed during the Thirty Years' War.

'Antique, irregular, picturesque', as Mary Shelley described it, Freiburg possesses all the charm of the Black Forest wine villages with the addition of students, a university and one of the finest cathedrals in Germany. Although much of the old city was destroyed by bombing on 27 November 1944, it has been lovingly reconstructed. Water flows everywhere. Along its narrow alleyways run rivulets known as *Bächle*, which carried away the sewage in medieval times. Towering above old Freiburg is the red sandstone minster with its dramatic spire, 116 metres tall – an octagonal belfry which becomes a lovely and intricate open-work *flèche*.

Freiburg cathedral was begun about 1200, some eighty years after Duke Konrad II of Zähringen founded the city. The architects were from the Basle guild of master masons. When Bertolt V, the last Duke of Zähringen, died in 1218, the romanesque part of the cathedral had already been completed and there he was buried. More than three centuries elapsed before the cathedral tower and choir were finished. Remarkably, at the time this majestic building was simply intended to be a parish church, not a cathedral, for Freiburg im Breisgau has been the seat of an archbishop only since 1827.

The sculptures around the main portal differ in one vital respect from those of the great cathedrals of northern France. In the latter the medieval iconography is invariably spread over several porches. At Freiburg all is confined to one doorway, resulting in a brilliantly complex piece of medieval art whose very compactness spells genius.

Inside the cathedral the splendid rose windows and the romanesque windows with round arches all date from the early thirteenth century, but the nave was not completed for another seventy years. The romanesque architects had crowned their work at the east end with a couple of towers. When the great gothic west tower was built, these two smaller ones were topped with little gothic spires to harmonize all

three. In Freiburg they are known as the *Hahnentürme* or cock-towers, from the shape of their weather vanes. In 1354 work began on building a huge choir around this romanesque shell. By 1380 its walls had reached a height of 5 metres and the side portals sculpted with scenes of the creation of the universe and the life of the Virgin Mary were finished. Then work stopped; the church had run out of money. Only in 1471 did the Emperor Maximilian I of Austria come to the rescue and pay for the completion of the dome of the choir.

This choir is entrancing, partly built by Johannes Parler who came from Gmünd in 1354 to begin the work, and completed after 1541 by an architect named Hans Niesenberger, who had the humility and intelligence to adhere to his predecessor's plans. In the central aisle are sculptures of Jesus and his apostles, chiselled between 1310 and 1330. Then your eye turns to gothic masterpieces: the pulpit, created by Jörg Kempf in 1561 (its canopy dates from 1795), with the carved *Madonna of the crescent moon* by Hans Wydz behind it; Hans Wydz's altar of the three kings in the transept, created in 1505; and above all the high altar, painted between 1512 and 1516 by Albrecht Dürer's pupil Hans Baldung Grien and depicting the coronation of the Virgin Mary.

This great building is suffused with light from the finest thirteenth- and fourteenth-century stained glass. Its sculptures are filled with enchantment. Seek out the carving at the entrance to the *Hahnentürm* chapel showing Alexander the Great falling out of a basket in which he is being borne to heaven by two griffins – a symbol of the punishment of human arrogance. Another favourite medieval symbol here is a wolf disguised as a monk. Instead of devoting himself to study and prayer, the wolf eats a lamb – a symbol of

Medieval stained glass in Freiburg cathedral adds to the ambience of one of the most exciting churches in Germany.

unfaithful clergy who prey on their flock rather than nurturing them.

I climbed the 328 steps of the cathedral tower, thankful that its 16 bronze bells were not ringing at the time. (The heaviest, weighing 5 tons and cast in 1258, rings every Friday at 11 o'clock.) On the way up you pass the quaint mechanism of the tower clock and there are stupendous views of the Black Forest and across the Rhine into France from the top. Or you can look down on the coloured umbrellas of the market, which takes place each morning (till one o'clock) in the Münsterplatz, and across to the half-renaissance, half-gothic Kaufhaus on the other side of the square. This intriguing building with two spiky towers at each corner is decorated with statues of Maximilian I, his son Philip I of Spain, and his grandsons Karl V and Ferdinand I. Built in 1532, it has one of the most picturesque courtyards in Germany.

The market in the cathedral square is laid out each day with remarkable precision. At the northern end farmers and their wives sell their own produce – vegetables, eggs, fruit. At the southern end you can buy ham and bacon, fruit, pottery (from Alsace as well as this region), honey and olives, woodcarvings and straw shoes. Flower-sellers have their stands west of the cathedral. During the last weekend of June the market is transformed for the annual wine festival and lined with the booths of vintners. Some 100,000 visitors cram into the city to taste and buy.

The episcopal palace, built in 1756 by the knights of Breisgau, stands in Münsterplatz. Only its baroque front survived World War II; the rest is a splendid post-war reconstruction, which today houses Benedictine nuns. Walk by three baroque columns (they represent the Virgin Mary, Bishop Lambertus and a saintly knight named Alexander) to reach Freiburg's oldest surviving fountain, the Fischbrunnen, which Hans von Basel created in 1483. A few metres away you can drink at the steeply gabled Ratskeller, once a cornmarket and banqueting hall, with a granary on the top floor. It looks for all the world as if it dates from the end of the fifteenth century, but in fact this Kornhaus is an exact copy, based on the original plans, of the 1497 building destroyed in November 1944.

Strolling west along Kaiser-Joseph-Strasse brings you to another interesting building, the delicately gabled yellow and pink Basler Hof, built around 1500. Statues of Emperor Heinrich II, a crowned Madonna, carrying her child and an orb, and Bishop Pantalus, all three of them patrons of the city, adorn its façade. When Freiburg bought its freedom from the earls of Urach in 1368 and voluntarily submitted to Austrian rule, this was the seat of the Austrian government for 300 years, till Louis XIV captured the city in 1677. Today a taste of this long Austrian rule is still discernible in Freiburg's cuisine, above all in its Linz almond tart. Wild boar from the Black Forest, pike rissoles from the River Dreisam, noodle after noodle are served in the handsome inns and *Weinstuben*, most of them decorated with window boxes of geraniums. Try a *Schäufele* or collar bone of pork, or a *Gugelhopf* angel cake. Freiburg has three breweries, so the beer is fresh and characteristically sharp. (The city's beer festival takes place in the week immediately following its wine festival.) Cherries, plums and damsons are transformed here into liqueurs known as Wässerli, and there is also a lethal brandy made from wild plums called Zibärtle.

Kaiser-Joseph-Strasse is an elegant pedestrianized shopping street, usually bustling and filled with street musicians and brass bandsmen in traditional costumes. Walk west along Schiffstrasse to the so-called potato market (Kartoffel-Markt), where you can buy not potatoes but silver, candles and leather goods. If you walk back to Kaiser-Joseph-Strasse and turn right into

---

Floral offerings in the market-place of Freiburg im Breisgau, for centuries an important crossroads in the Rhine valley.

Franziskanerstrasse you reach the exquisite late gothic House of the Whale (*Haus zum Walfisch*), all pink except for the delicately carved alcove and doorway picked out in gold. Kaiser Maximilian I's treasurer Jakob Villinger von Schönenberg built it in 1516. Here Erasmus of Rotterdam took refuge in 1529 when at length he found the religious climate of Basle inhospitable.

Walk on to the town hall square, shaded by chestnuts, where the fountain bears a monument to Berthold Schwarz. This Franciscan friar is credited with inventing gunpowder in 1353, a strange legacy to humanity from a supposed follower of the prince of peace. The town hall is actually two buildings, a couple of sixteenth-century houses linked by arcades built in 1901. The pavement in front of the arcades is decorated with mosaics of the coats of arms of four foreign cities twinned with Freiburg – Guildford in Britain, Besançon in France, Innsbruck in Austria and Padua in Italy – and in front of the older building is a mosaic of Freiburg's own coat of arms. Go inside the courtyard of the town hall to admire the spiral staircase of 1588, twisting up its tower. On a gabled building to the left, built in 1600, is the double-headed Habsburg eagle. If you arrive at the town hall at three minutes past noon, a *Glockenspiel* regales you with folksongs.

The church of St Martin in this square was begun by Franciscan friars in 1262. The present apparently thirteenth-century building – simple, austere and beautiful – in truth dates from 1953, a faithful reconstruction of the original after the former church was utterly demolished by the bombs of World War II. When the city architects re-created it, they chose to abolish all the later additions, save for the 1719 'Sunday portal'.

Another impressive church, dedicated to St Ursula

The superb wrought-iron gate of the *Haus zum Walfisch*, **Freiburg, dates only from 1911.**

and with an interior finished in 1719, stands at the end of the Rathausgasse (to the left of the new town hall), a narrow street washed by one of the *Bächle* and with some dated medieval buildings: *Zum Biber* (the beaver's house) of 1460; *Zum Geilen Fisch* (the merry fish) of 1390; *Zum Blauen Sperber* (the blue sparrow-hawk) of roughly the same date. Beyond the church a pedestrian subway in front of the tourist office leads to a park which still boasts a tiny vineyard and where you can picnic in peace. The nineteenth-century gothic castle here, picturesquely festooned in vines and with roses and shrubs creeping up to its doors, houses Freiburg's prehistory museum.

Several streets in this evocative city recall the trades of those who once occupied them. Stroll past the Martinstor, one of the city's two surviving thirteenth-century gates (the other one, the Schwabentor, houses a museum of model tin figures), and turn left into the Fischerau. More a stream than a street, this is where the city's fishermen once lived. The nearby Gerberau with its antique shops and steeply gabled houses is named after the tanners who once made it the centre of their trade. Close by is the Metzgerau, once the preserve of Freiburg's butchers. Follow Gerberau and you reach the ochre-coloured walls of the former Augustinian monastery housing some of the greatest treasures of German art, such as paintings by Baldung and Grünewald and romanesque and gothic stained glass, in its late thirteenth-century church, its cloisters and its great hall. Opposite the monastery stands a palace built for the Grand Duke by Pierre Michel d'Ixnard in 1773.

The Oberlinden district by the Schwabentor boasts a lime tree that has been growing here for two and a half centuries and a square graced by a baroque fountain in honour of the Virgin Mary. If you walk from here through Herrenstrasse you reach Münsterplatz by way of the Präsengässle. At the corner of the square graceful ironwork and a balcony identify the aptly named 'house on the beautiful corner' (*Haus zum*

Berthold Schwarz, the monk who invented gunpowder, is commemorated in a statue in Freiburg's town-hall square (*right*), and in this sculpture (*above*), where he recoils in horror from his invention.

Schönen Eck), designed by Christian Wenziger in 1761.

One delight of this city is its friendly mountain, the Schauinsland, some 1000 metres higher than the cathedral square. Drive up to its peak by the winding road that is used as a race track once a year, or take the cable-car from the suburb of Horben. From the top of the mountain you can see across to the Vosges on the other side of the Rhine, and on clear days it is even possible to pick out the Zugspitze and Mont Blanc in the Alps to the east.

Yet more rewarding is to make an excursion from Freiburg to see some of the most stupendous scenery of the Black Forest and its two greatest lakes: Titisee and Schluchsee. The road runs south-east along the River Dreisam past the eighteenth-century *Schloss* at Ebnet and climbs up through a string of lovely little villages. After Falkensteig, with its ruined old castle, it plunges into the overwhelmingly magnificent Höllenpass or Hell's valley, where the great bronze figure of a stag celebrates a noble beast that is said to have escaped its hunters by leaping across this ravine. A little further on you pass the oldest surviving religious house in the Black Forest, the St-Oswald-Kapelle, consecrated in 1154. Not surprisingly the superb scenery and the clear mountain air have led to the growth of winter sports and health centres at Oberhöllsteig and Hinzerzarten, from where the road starts to descend to Lake Titisee itself.

Even the tourist shops selling horrendous cuckoo-clocks and other trinkets cannot spoil the natural beauty of this mountain-ringed serene stretch of water, where you can swim and sail. The little town of Titisee at the northern end is an excellent starting-point for excursions into the Black Forest with its highest peak, the 1493-metre Feldberg, not far to the south.

Deep among the Black Forest pines, where a sturdy farmhouse or half-timbered village suddenly offers a glimpse of time past.

If anything the journey from Freiburg is most spectacular in winter. The sparse firs often fail to shake off the snow; and the tourist industry ensures that you can still drive along the roads. Or you can enjoy the scenery from the rack railway through the Höllenpass. Schluchsee to the south is another beauty spot, reached by following the road along the west shore of Lake Titisee and turning sharply left at Bärental (which boasts the highest station on the West German railways).

Returning to Freiburg, take the B31 through Umkirch (with a romantic *Schloss*), and Ihringen (which claims to be Germany's warmest town) to the astonishing, virtually unknown frontier town of Breisach, standing bold and dominating on a steep promontory overlooking the Rhine. Drive around its sixteenth-century fortifications to reach the Rhine gate built by Vauban when Louis XIV claimed the town, decorated with medallions depicting the Sun King and his queen. Park in the square and walk up to the mighty grey-walled minster of St Stephen, a massive basilica whose two towers, one gothic, the other romanesque, indicate that this church was built over 300 years, from the early thirteenth to the late fifteenth century. An extraordinary carving on the vestry door depicts the martyrdom of St Mauritius and the Theban Legion, all of whom, according to legend, opted for Jesus rather than paganism and were slain for their faith. Martyrdoms gave devout sculptors the excuse to indulge their most sadistic fantasies, and here the opportunity has been seized enthusiastically. Thorns pierce the legionaries; their intestines protrude; their heads are savagely removed with one stroke of a sword.

The interior of the minster is also outstanding, with a superb gothic rood screen and an intricately carved limewood high altar of 1526 by (I think) Hans Loi. By general agreement, Tilman Riemenschneider of Bavaria is the greatest limewood sculptor of all time, and I have seen much (if not all) of his work. Believe me, this

work by Hans Loi equals it. The curling beard of God the Father is wild and yet godly. St John the Apostle serenely writes his gospel, ringlets falling on either side of his devout face, a fierce eagle holding up his book which, in the manner of all important sixteenth-century books, has a clasp and a lock.

As with the exterior, romanesque and gothic are mingled here, with a high gothic choir set within an overall romanesque design. Piers and vaults give an impression of loftiness rarely matched in Germany. One of the most distinctive features of the church is the terrifying Doom painted on its walls between 1488 and 1491 by Martin Schongauer of Colmar. On the south wall he depicted the saints ecstatically received into heaven. Across the west wall, enthroned upon a rainbow, Christ pronounces judgment. On the north wall vicious creatures, half-beast, half-human, drag the damned to hell. As if to make up for this frightful vision, the minster is surrounded by a peaceful garden

---

Romanesque and renaissance in Breisach, a border town where the road to Colmar crosses the Rhine from Germany.

where you can sit quietly, drinking in the subtle changes in the views across the Rhine, watching the mist rising gently from the water in autumn and winter.

Leave Breisach through a gateway built in 1541 from where a wooden bridge over the city moat leads to the Rhine gate. On your left is the Kaiserstuhl, a volcanic mountain covered in vines and exotic plants and alive with butterflies in summer, once supposed to be the temporary resting-place of the Emperor Friedrich Barbarossa, drowned in Palestine in 1190 while on a crusade, but awaiting his call to come to earth again. From here the road runs south-east for 15 kilometres to Bad Krozingen, where there is a warm therapeutic spring said to cure rheumatism, gout, lumbago and heart diseases and the inevitable *Schloss*, built here in 1579. Müllheim to the south brings a touch of France, with a cuisine featuring snails, as well as the German delights of horseradish, liver, kidneys and celery. To add to these charms, Müllheim is also the centre of the wine trade of this region, with the produce of local vineyards on offer to drink with a picnic lunch sitting in the shade on the north side of St Martin's church. From Müllheim the road runs due south back to Basle.

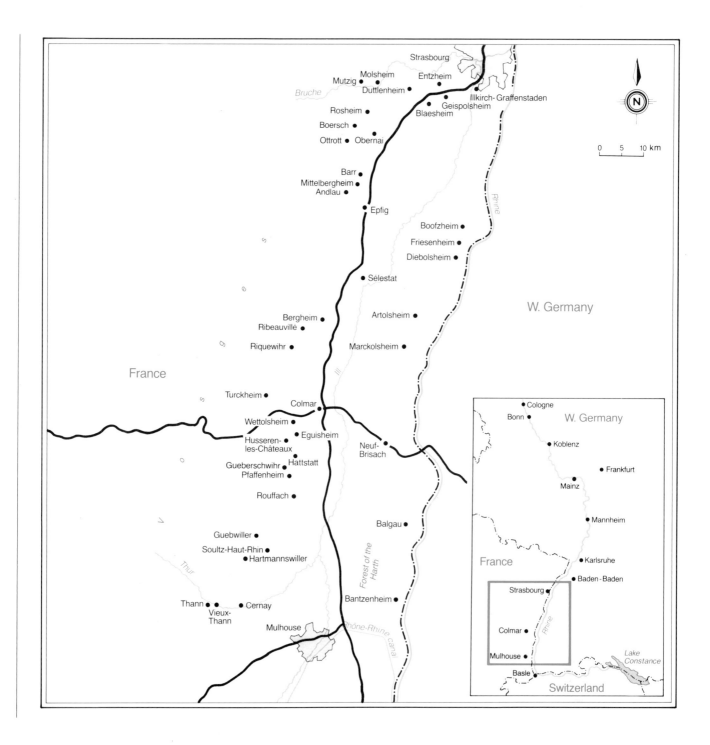

Strasbourg
Mutzig • • Molsheim • Entzheim
Bruche • Duttlenheim
• Illkirch-Graffenstaden
Rosheim • Geispolsheim
Boersch • Blaesheim
Ottrott • • Obernai

Barr •
Mittelbergheim •
Andlau •
Epfig •
Boofzheim •
Friesenheim •
Diebolsheim •
Sélestat •

W. Germany

Bergheim •
Ribeauvillé •
Riquewihr •

Artolsheim •

Marckolsheim •

France

Turckheim •
Colmar •
Wettolsheim •
Eguisheim •
Husseren- •
les-Châteaux
Gueberschwihr • • Hattstatt
Pfaffenheim •
Neuf- •
Brisach
Rouffach •

Balgau •

Guebwiller •
Soultz-Haut-Rhin •
• Hartmannswiller

Forest of the Harth

Thann • •
Vieux-
Thann
• Cernay
Bantzenheim •

Mulhouse

Rhône-Rhine canal

Thur

0   5   10 km

N

Cologne •
Bonn •
W. Germany
Koblenz •
Frankfurt •
Mainz •
Mannheim •
France
Karlsruhe •
Baden-Baden •
Strasbourg •
Colmar •
Mulhouse •
Basle •
Switzerland
Lake Constance
Rhine

2
Where
Germany embraces France

*Colmar – Eguisheim – Rouffach – Guebwiller –
Cernay – Thann – Mulhouse – Neuf-Brisach –
Geispolsheim – Molsheim – Obernai – Barr –
Sélestat – Ribeauvillé – Riquewihr*

Between the River Rhine and the Vosges lies the frontier province of Alsace, its troubled history reflected in ruined châteaux and the fortifications that picturesquely surround many of the old towns and villages. In western Alsace, the lower slopes of the forested Vosges are criss-crossed with the vines that produce the world-renowned Alsatian wines. By contrast, the fertile plain extending along the Rhine to the border with Switzerland in the south supports cereals, sugar beet, fruit trees and cattle.

In the many richly carved restaurants and cafés which are such a feature of this region, some of them still warmed by old-fashioned tiled stoves, you would be forgiven for asking whether you were in Germany or France. Since World War II, when it was occupied by the forces of Adolf Hitler, Alsace has been French, but many legacies of earlier periods of German rule remain and the culture of this unique area reflects both French and German influences. At the same time it is totally individual. The cuisine served here draws on both French and German roots, but long ago developed its own distinctive character. Steep-roofed houses, overhanging balconies profusely decorated with begonias in summer, huge storks' nests on the church towers and the town gates and exquisite fountains all contribute to a fairy-tale atmosphere. Alsatians believe that the storks bring them good luck. Each September the birds migrate with their young to Africa, returning in March to repair their nests and raise their young.

The vintners of Alsace have created a wine road which runs for 120 kilometres from Obernai in the north to Thann in the south, lined with stalls and cellars where you are invited to sample the produce and then buy half a dozen bottles. On either side vineyards stretch away into the distance, merging into woodland on far horizons. In summer the people of the region sit under parasols by the roadside, selling their home-produced honey as well as wine. This part of Alsace always reminds me of a beautifully-kept garden.

Colmar on the River Ill should be the start of any tour of this region. Of the twenty guilds or corporations here at the end of the seventeenth century, the greatest was that of the vintners, with a staggering 700 members. Even so these 700 owned but 350 of the 500 hectares of land around the city given over to vines. The rest belonged to other vintners, to the city's convents and churches and to noble families who hired others to tend them. By this time Colmar had long been an imperial city, granted the right to mint its own money in the late fourteenth century and boasting a democratic constitution that lasted from 1361 until 1648. Riches based on trade were enhanced by the wealth of religious art created by the Franciscans, Cistercians and other orders who established themselves here. Yet Colmar remained and remains to this day a city on a human scale.

Where you find fine wines, you eat fine food, and Colmar is no exception to this rule. Writing about Alsace in 1811, the celebrated gastronome Brillat-Savarin confessed that it was 'one of the regions of Europe that has most stirred my taste-buds', bluntly declaring that he had scarcely ever salivated so much elsewhere. Brillat-Savarin, like most great gastronomes, was a Frenchman, but here he was praising a French cuisine deeply influenced by Germany. The menu that was offered on New Year's Eve 1987 by Patrick Fulgraff at the restaurant Fer Rouge in Colmar perfectly exemplifies this fact. It read:

Huitres à la crème
Foies d'oie à la choucroute
Pot-au-feu d'escargots
Noix de Saint-Jacques au pinot noir
Mille-feuilles aux pommes

Apart from the oysters, which every French family eats in abundance to welcome a new year, and the *foies d'oie*, which you would also expect to find in the Dordogne, the dishes on offer were traditional Alsatian cuisine whose essence remains essentially Germanic. Germany embraces France in Alsatian food as well as in the history of this much fought-over province.

Maître Fulgraff's *foies d'oie* served with sauerkraut brilliantly combined what is traditionally thought of as a French delicacy with a German vegetable. In fact the *foie gras* of Alsace is as famous as that of the Dordogne, although it was brought here by the French after the Treaty of Westphalia ceded the province to France in 1648. Envious of the cuisine of the officials who came to run their land, the Alsatian nobility hired their own French chefs. In 1780 Jean-Pierre Clause, *chef-de-cuisine* to the governor of Alsace, Marshal de Contades, packed a pastry crust with *foie gras* and cunningly named his dish after his master. The governor was delighted and sent a gift of *pâté de Contades* to Louis XVI. The king was entranced. *Foie gras d'Alsace* had become a national dish. Today Alsatian restaurants almost always marinate *foie gras* in sparkling wine overnight, before encasing it in pastry and serving it cold as *brioche de foie gras*, sometimes laced with game stock.

The over-sensitive shudder at the fact that *foie gras* is created by force-feeding geese to make their livers swell and become extraordinarily succulent. In fact, were they able to, the geese would force-feed themselves, which is how *foie gras* was initially discovered. The Romans saw that these enthusiastically greedy fowl even ate rotting apples and other fallen fruit. When they killed them for dinner, the geese had livers the size of a plucked chicken. The birds had lived well and their owners subsequently dined well. I comfort myself with such thoughts in autumn, when I visit Alsace markets packed with stalls selling this extremely expensive delicacy.

The observant may, however, notice that there are not many geese in this part of France and wonder where the delicacy comes from. It is a well-kept secret that *foie gras* in Alsace is scarcely ever obtained from local geese, of which there are few, but usually imported, mostly from Hungary. If you read the words *foie gras maison* on a menu, do not expect the chef to have force-fed his own geese. The legend means that he has prepared it after his own fashion.

The sauerkraut, or *choucroute*, with which Patrick Fulgraff accompanied his dish is usually eaten in

Bustling Colmar, whose ancient buildings and lovely art galleries make it one of the most attractive cities in Alsace.

An inn sign at Colmar celebrates a famous son of Alsace, Napoleon's doughty General Kléber, who was assassinated at Cairo in 1800, aged only 47.

it with them. Alsace took to it with relish.

An ancient Alsace proverb declares, 'Eat and drink well, and you will keep love and your soul in harmony.' With the oysters Patrick Fulgraff recommended his customers to drink a glass or two of that wine known as pinot blanc, which Alsatians call Klevner. With the snail dish he offered his guests a bottle of straw-coloured Alsace Riesling, made from one of the three main varieties of grape grown in Alsace. Its special Alsatian tang, which vintners describe as virile, proud or round, is derived from the sunny and unusually chalky slopes on which it grows. The main meat course was accompanied with a bottle of pinot noir. Like pinot gris, pinot noir is cursed with a quaint adjective. 'Noir' means black, but pinot noir is not at all black. This wine is a gentle, opulent half-red, half-rosé wine. With his *foies d'oie à la choucroute* Maître Fulgraff recommended his patrons to drink a wine known as tokay d'Alsace. Strictly speaking he should not have used that name, for in 1984 headstrong officialdom decreed that tokay d'Alsace should henceforth be called pinot gris. 'Gris', the French for 'grey', seems to me a foolish adjective to use of a wine, suggesting some milk and water concoction. The truth is that tokay d'Alsace (or pinot gris) is a golden white wine and, unlike the delicate pinot blanc, heady and strong, a perfect accompaniment to any *foie gras* or meat dish more usually complemented by a red wine.

Colmar has long been renowned not simply for its wine producers but also for its wine drinkers. In the Middle Ages clubs of wine-bibbers would gather round their tiled stoves in the evening to sample the local vintages. The word for stoves is *poêles* and these clubs became known by the same name: *poêles*. They would pool their resources to buy the best products of the local vintners, setting themselves up in distinguished fraternities, some of which survive to this day. These confraternities developed elaborate and exclusive rules, as well as delightful rituals, but the chief

Alsace with boiled potatoes and slices of pork, or else with bacon and grilled sausages of the most pungent kind. If you are offered *choucroute royale*, the accompanying meats and sausages are far more than I can eat. The astringent cabbage is very rarely offered as a delicate bed for *foie gras*, as on the New Year's Eve menu at the Fer Rouge. Like many other foods, sauerkraut is also redolent with history. In his *foies d'oie à la choucroute* Maître Fulgraff happened to marry a French speciality with one derived from China. The sauerkraut plant was first cultivated by the Chinese as sustenance for those who toiled building the Great Wall. When the Tartars invaded Europe they brought

qualification for membership was always a desire to drink quantities of wine, albeit with discrimination. The most famous such fraternity in Alsace is the Confraternity of St Stephen (or Saint-Étienne), which has a wine museum at Kientzheim just outside Colmar. You can find it by following the signs pointing out of the city to Strasbourg along the route du 152e Regiment de Infanterie. Then turn left along the route des Francs and right along avenue de la Foire au Vins and you are there. There is plenty of parking space. An old wine press adorns the courtyard, and inside you can see the implements used in wine-making for centuries.

The Fer Rouge stands in the oldest and most attractive part of the city, flanked by two elegant seventeenth-century houses, one arcaded, the other with a splendid oriel window. These are but two of the many handsome buildings that are a legacy of Colmar's long history as a trading city. Arguably the finest of all is the former customs house, or 'Koïfhus', at one end of the Grand'Rue. Its tiled roof is decorated with green lozenges, and in summer its balconies are ablaze with flowers. As an inscription carried by an angel carved on the façade of this elegant arcaded building proclaims, it was built in 1480, intended as much more than a warehouse. Colmar was the strongest of the ten imperial cities in Alsace which formed a defensive alliance called the Decapolis in 1354, and it was agreed that the representatives of each city should meet in its Koïfhus. Today you can see the coat of arms of each city of the alliance glowing in the stained-glass windows on the first floor. The double-headed eagle over the gothic doorways represents the Holy Roman Empire.

Pass through the graceful arcades of the Koïfhus (noting the victory column set up in 1543 to mark the defeat of the Prince of Clèves by Charles V) into the place de l'Ancienne Douane. The splendid fountain here was created by the distinguished Auguste Bartholdi, born in Colmar in 1834, who is much better known for the famous Statue of Liberty which greets every ship coming into the port of New York. The figure depicted on this fountain is the sixteenth-century Habsburg general Lazarus de Schwendi, who has a legendary place in Alsace wine lore. Tradition has it that he spotted the virtues of the pinot gris grape while fighting in Hungary and brought the plant back to Alsace. Alas, this attractive legend is not born out by the facts. The golden wine had always been made here from a grape descended from the old French Furmint variety. None the less Lazarus de Schwendi was certainly a good man, one capable of such a benefaction. After his fighting days were over he installed himself in the château at Kientzheim which is

This entrancing fifteenth-century ironwork on the door of Colmar's former customs house is matched by the delicacy of the coloured tiles of its roof.

now the home of the Colmar wine confraternity of Saint-Étienne and devoted himself in those troubled times to the task of reconciling Catholics and Protestants.

Only a stone's throw from the Koïfhus is an unexpected and entrancing water-lapped district of Colmar known as Little Venice, reached along the rue des Tanneurs, a street of late fifteenth- and sixteenth-century houses from Colmar's golden age. Little Venice itself is a watery warren of pretty streets and half-timbered houses, many with balconies looking out on to the River Lauch.

On the south side of the river the place des Six-Montagnes-Noirs displays a monument to Rosselmann, provost of Colmar in the thirteenth century, by Bartholdi. The birthplace of this famous nineteenth-century sculptor is not far from here, again reached along some of Colmar's most enchanting streets. Turn right along rue Saint-Jean, where the knights of St John built a house in 1608 in the Venetian style, ornamented with gargoyles and balustrades. At the Koïfhus turn left along rue des Marchands. This magical street includes the gothic maison Adolphe, Colmar's oldest house, built in 1340, with a well at its corner dated 1592 that was brought here in 1931. By contrast, the house next door was built in 1706 and boasts classical pillars and arcades. On the other side of the street three houses in succession date from the fifteenth and sixteenth centuries.

No. 30, rue des Marchands, is the house where Auguste Bartholdi was born and today serves as his museum. His cluttered Paris apartment has been reconstructed on the first floor, displaying his furniture and scale-models of his works; the second floor is called the Statue of Liberty room and contains fascinating plans and documents relating to that masterpiece.

Close by the maison Adolphe you can see the church of Saint-Martin, known as the cathedral of Colmar because of its splendour and dimensions. Originally built between 1237 and 1366, its lovely bell-tower was added after a fire in 1572. Walk round the building to admire the carvings on the doorways. Maître Humbret, architect of the nave, is portrayed on the south doorway. Just inside, a picture on the left shows bluebirds perching in golden trees, with the Infant Jesus holding one of them in his hand. He stands upright, a major feat for such a young child. The interior of this great church is rich in sculpted bosses and statues, of which the finest are possibly a fourteenth-century crucifixion and the fifteenth-century *Virgin of Colmar*. The octagonal choir built by Guillaume de Marburg in 1366 contains magnificently carved stalls. Two fourteenth-century stained-glass windows include ten panels depicting scenes from the medieval mystical treatise *The Mirror of Our Salvation*. And there is an organ-case by the Silbermann brothers, whom many experts judge to be the greatest organ builders of the eighteenth century.

In 1927 the American stained-glass buff Charles Hitchcock Sherrill visited the church and enthused over a window depicting the patron saint arrayed in his robes as Bishop of Tours and 'engaged in the cheery task of leading a skeleton by the hand'. Sherrill was very interested to hear the local rumour that the Austrian General von Frimont had taken several chests of ancient glass from the church in 1715 and that he was made to send some of it back. 'If this be true', mused Sherrill, 'it would be interesting to locate the rest of the loot in Austria.' Unfortunately, he never pursued the idea further.

Many of the carvings on the houses of Colmar rival those to be seen in this church. To enjoy some of the

---

A willow overhangs the waters of the River Lauch in Colmar's Little Venice, a quiet quarter of the city, once the home of market gardeners, where the atmosphere of tranquillity is irresistible.

best, walk from St Martin through the thirteenth-century arcades back into rue des Marchands again, turning left to see the bearded man carved on the corner of Zum Kragen in 1419. Directly opposite the church the maison Adolphe is flanked by the prettiest house in the city, the maison Pfister, built in 1527, painted and renewed in 1599 and restored in 1971. Its powerful overhanging balcony dates from 1577, added on to the house built some forty years earlier by a prosperous Colmar draper. The façade is carved and painted with themes from the Bible and representations of the seven virtues as well as displaying the heads of Charles V and Maximilian of Austria. The house next door is engraved with the date 1609.

On the corner opposite is a half-timbered house built in 1373, the home of the talented Schongauer family from 1465 to 1583. The father of the household was a goldsmith from Augsburg. Of his four sons, three were skilled painters and goldsmiths, but the most gifted was the painter Martin, who was born in this house. After studying at the university of Leipzig and in the studio of the Flemish master Roger van der Weyden the Elder, Martin returned to Colmar where he produced most of his finest works. Here too he founded a school of brilliant engravers. In 1473 he created his masterpiece, the *Madonna in the Rose Garden*. It shuttles between the church of St Martin and the church of the Dominicans, so I cannot tell you precisely where to find it. I also wish I could explain why he has dressed the Virgin Mary in red rather than her normal blue. Two angels descending to place a golden crown on her head wear the Virgin's traditional colour.

The graceful spire of the slender Dominican church comes into sight as you walk to the end of rue des Marchands. Rudolph von Habsburg laid its foundation stone in 1283, but the church was not finished till the eighteenth century. The oldest part is the choir, completed in 1310, and the superb stained glass also dates from the fourteenth century. The adjoining convent buildings are now the city library.

Take rue des Boulangers into rue des Têtes from here to see the delightful maison des Têtes, a three-storeyed house of 1609 carved with innumerable heads – hence its name. The renaissance gable is topped by a statue of a cooper by Bartholdi, bottle in one hand and a glass in the other. Today the maison des Têtes is the headquarters of the wine merchants of the city, who took over the house in 1898 and now run it as an excellent restaurant. Inside the archway two more chubby heads turn out to be those of Gustave Burger and Louis Nortmeyer. These Alsatian vintners were instrumental in reviving the trade after it had fallen into disrepute when Alsace was occupied by Germany between 1871 and 1918. There is also an effigy of the devil, disguised as a jester. His cloven hoofs are visible, but he is fortunately bound in a strait-jacket with his legs tied together.

Rue des Têtes will lead you to perhaps the most important reason for visiting Colmar: the Unterlinden Museum, housed in the former monastery of St John beneath the lime trees – hence *Unterlinden* – which was founded by pious women dedicated to the rule of St Dominic and consecrated by St Albert the Great, Bishop of Regensburg, in 1269. The monastery was dissolved at the Revolution, but its exquisite buildings were bought in 1850 by the Schongauer Society of Colmar and turned into a museum and art gallery. The cloister with its 54 arcades supported by twin pillars is a work of art in itself. The displays include romanesque sculptures and stone tombs, gothic masterpieces and magical paintings by Gaspard Isenmann and Martin Schongauer, and a cellar filled with archaeological finds and twentieth-century works of art. But what brings crowds here is a nine-panelled altarpiece in the chapel: the Isenheim triptych by Mathias Grünewald.

Scarcely anything is known about this artist, except that he was born around 1460 at Würzburg and died at Halle in 1528. His real name was Mathias Gothard Neithart, and he worked for the archbishops of Mainz and Magdeburg. Fifty years after his death the German Joachim von Sandrart wrote that 'He led a lonely and melancholy life, and was unhappily married.' After his death a nailed-up chest that he had owned was found to contain a Bible in German and some of the treatises of Luther. Grünewald evidently sympathized with the Reformation. Yet his art seems to me to derive essentially from medieval mysticism, combined with a realism which made him (so experts surmise) use bodies from mortuaries as models for his paintings of Jesus dead on the cross.

His Christ hanging on the cross in the Unterlinden Museum is horrific, rotting, open-mouthed and utterly dead. Grünewald painted it for the monks of St Anthony, Isenheim, who ran a hospital for those suffering from gangrene, epilepsy and other incurable diseases. This crucified Jesus is also gangrenous, bloated and mottled with sores. To his right the Virgin Mary swoons into the arms of St John. In front of them St Mary Magdalen kneels in prayer, her tormented hands clasped in mute appeal to her Lord. To his left St John the Baptist points at the dead Jesus, exclaiming 'He must increase and I must decrease', words taken from the New Testament. Other panels depict St Sebastian pierced by arrows, scenes from the life of St Anthony (including a terrifying attack on him by demons), prophets, archangels, a lovely annunciation scene, an ecstatic portrait of the Virgin and Child (with angels making music) and a yet more ecstatic resurrection.

Leave Colmar by way of the avenue de la Liberté and the route de Munster, and take the N83 south towards Eguisheim, through the wine village of Wettolsheim. Eguisheim was curiously designed in the form of an ellipse and is still protected by its thirteenth-century fortifications, a perfect circuit for a Sunday afternoon stroll. This was the birthplace of Pope Leo IX, who reigned from 1048 to 1054 and longed to reunite the eastern and western church. Alas, his papacy saw the final rift between them. His statue stands on a fountain

Ancient shuttered Turckheim just outside Colmar, one of Alsace's gems, crammed with historic houses, surrounded by vineyards and washed by the River Fecht.

in the middle of the village, surrounded by fine vintners' houses and tithe barns fronting great courtyards, and overlooked by three ruined châteaux. Although the church of St Peter and St Paul was rebuilt in 1807, one of the old romanesque doorways still survives, ornamented with fine carvings of Jesus and the two patron saints, accompanied by the wise and foolish virgins. The belfry is gothic.

The little village of Husseren-les-Châteaux a short distance away is dominated by three medieval towers. Once there were three châteaux, but a disgruntled youth from Mulhouse called Hermann Klee, annoyed at being cheated of six *deniers* by his employers, burned them down in 1466. From here drive south to Hattstatt with its pretty sixteenth-century town hall

Above An Eguisheim cat relishes the entrancing streets of a town which produced the only Alsatian pope, Leo IX, and 900 years later still preserves the medieval charm of his era.

Right The romanesque tower of Gueberschwihr church, fortified like the village itself, is today set among lovely vintners' houses.

The romanesque doorway of the church of Our Lady, Rouffach, begun at the end of the eleventh century, enlarged by the great medieval gothic architects and finished only a hundred years ago.

(boasting a double external staircase) and renaissance houses, and turn off west to Gueberschwihr, another fortified village full of picturesque vintners' houses, some of them built of sandstone, others half-timbered. Coats of arms pontificate over many doorways. Here another nineteenth-century church incorporates part of an earlier building, in this case the exquisite romanesque bell-tower. Its three sets of lights are in delicate harmony with each other, rising from two twin windows through three twin windows to two triple windows.

Continue along the D1V and you reach Pfaffenheim, another wine village with a nineteenth-century church, but in this case sporting a twentieth-century bell-tower. Although you may not think it worth looking inside, this unpromising building conceals a late thirteenth-century choir which is both simple and totally satisfying.

A much more splendid building dominates Rouffach, 9 kilometres from Eguisheim. This exceptional church has a twelfth- and thirteenth-century central tower, 68 metres high, flanked by slightly lower towers on either side built in the fourteenth and nineteenth centuries. That on the left is 56 metres high, that on the right, still unfinished, is several metres lower, so the whole façade looks quaintly out of balance. Thirteenth-century doorways and a rose window add to the glory of the building. It stands in a picturesque group with the sixteenth-century double gabled renaissance town hall and the gabled corn market of 1569 with its external staircase.

I never went to church in Rouffach, but I was told that if you do you will find the women sitting on the right-hand side, in the places normally reserved for men. This privilege dates from 1106 when the future Holy Roman Emperor Heinrich V lived in Rouffach château and his aides terrorized everyone. The citizens threw him and his servants out of the town, having stolen the royal insignia. The enraged Heinrich came back and set fire to Rouffach. By now the men were fearful, but the women once again expelled their insolent lord. Their reward is enjoyed to this day. Next to the church stands an arrogant handsome statue of Napoleon's general François-Joseph Lefebre, born here in 1756. Orphaned, he was brought up by the parish priest at Guémar, and became a member of the French Guard in Paris by the time he was eighteen. Lefebre was commanding his own brigades by 1794 and became military governor of Paris five years later. He fought valiantly at the battle of Danzig in 1807 and again at Moscow in 1815. He deserves his statue.

Also in the middle of the town is the tour des Sorcières, topped by a storks' nest. Earlier this century these symbols of good fortune seemed to be dying out in Alsace. Many migrated in winter and never came back. The population decreased to the point where, in 1932, there were only 132 pairs and around 400 young storks in the whole region. Since then the Alsatians have made determined efforts to encourage the storks to breed, setting up platforms to attract them, and have repopulated their towns (although it must be said that this only applies to white storks – the Alsatians neglect the seventeen other species).

The American writer Gertrude Stein, who liked the storks but disliked the Alsace patois, once declared that 'Their storks are their statuettes', adding that 'The Alsatians do not sing as well as their storks.' As an example of the locals' quaint tongue, she invented some doggerel verse which (she claimed) sounded like the Alsatian dialect:

> Now we come back to the Schemmils.
> Schimmel, Schimmel, Gott in Himmel,
> Gott in Himmel! Here comes Schimmel,
> Schimmel is an Alsatian name.

There is nothing in that diatribe to remind me of what I hear in an Alsatian *Winstub*, which is itself patois for *Weinstube*. These slightly lighter versions of a German pub have similarly heavy furniture and, as in Germany, the host will have his own table or *Stammtisch*, usually beautifully carved. Here only the favoured guests of the landlord or landlady can sit, and only by invitation. But everyone is welcome to drink either Alsatian wine or Alsatian beer.

It was in one of these friendly places in Rouffach that I fell ill of the gripe. *La grippe intestinale* simply means gastric flu, but I think it sounds better (or rather, worse) in French. Returning to my hotel, for a time I simply coughed and spluttered over everyone, hoping that what I was suffering from would go away and attempting to work on with increasing lassitude. A guest at the hotel came up with a remedy. He persuaded the landlady to warm some wine to which

Guebwiller's dolphin fountain, only one of the treasures in a town which boasts a spectacular town hall and three magnificent churches.

he added lemons and cinnamon. Then he poked an iron into the open fire, took it out red-hot and plunged it into the mixture. He called the potion *vin ferré*. Though it did not cure me, the medicine certainly made me feel much better. That evening I comforted myself with a typical Alsace meal of beer soup (or *Biersupp*, containing diced onions, chicken stock, croûtons, fresh cream and a third of a litre of light ale), followed by *le Bäeckaoffa* – a hearty casserole of meat, potatoes and onions. To keep my strength up, the following morning I breakfasted on the regional speciality known as *Kougelhopf*, a rich concoction of raisins, almonds, sugar and eggs, sprinkled with icing sugar, which is baked in a specially-moulded dish that produces a twisting pattern rather like a jelly.

So I drove on to Guebwiller, 8 kilometres south, just in time to catch Alfred Brendel giving a recital of Haydn, Schumann and Franz Liszt in the former Dominican church. Begun in 1312, this great building is decorated with fourteenth- and fifteenth-century frescoes. The vineyards around Guebwiller are a labour of love, beautifully stepped up the hillsides. Another church, Notre-Dame, is a half-classical, half-baroque delight of 1785, with two rows of pillars, the bottom ones Doric, the top ones Corinthian in style. Its architect was Louis Beuque from Besançon, aided by the sculptor Gabriel-Ignace Ritter. A fine classical belfry and clock-tower rise from the right-hand corner of the façade. The interior is splendid, very Corinthian baroque. Around the dome sit the four doctors of the church, carved by Ritter. On the baroque high altar Our Lady ascends to heaven, in a carving by Fidèle-Joseph Sporer, watched by the eye of God set in a triangle above. The stalls depict scenes from the Old Testament: Elijah calling down fire on his own sacrifice and the pursuers of Moses and the children of Israel about to be drowned in the Red Sea. Among the New Testament scenes is a carving of the brilliant young Jesus absolutely lording it over the elders in the Temple at Jerusalem. Jesus is helped by the guidance of the Holy Spirit, whose inspiration falls like drops of water. Another carving, of the Nativity, includes a sheep asleep in the foreground, its legs crossed, and a goose in a basket.

Left of the church stands the abbot's château, a powerfully arrogant building designed by Peter Thumb in 1715. The canons' houses are grouped round about, not so splendid as the abbot's home but still fine enough, and all dating from the second half of the eighteenth century. They all have a good view of the splendid dolphin fountain in front of the church.

Guebwiller also possesses a third magnificent church, the romanesque Saint-Léger. Half-way between it and the Dominican church is a town hall built in 1514 which has a five-sided oriel window and a delicate staircase. Walk along the rue de la République for yet more fine houses. If you can, plan to come here on Ascension Day, when the town celebrates its wine festival.

The road to Soultz-Haut-Rhin runs from the north side of the church of Notre-Dame. 'You will be astounded at the fertility and the divine bounty of this land', wrote the humanist Sebastian Franck in 1534, 'which not only nourishes its whole population but also permits almost the whole world to drink its wines.' Barges along the River Rhine were the means of transporting these wines, taking them to Germany, to Holland, to the Hanseatic ports and to England. Soultz-Haut-Rhin perfectly exemplifies the golden age of Alsatian building that was based on the riches created by this trade. Although the little town suffered damage in World War I, its fine sixteenth- and seventeenth-century houses have mostly been beautifully restored and are in splendid condition today. So is its gothic church of Saint-Maurice (which houses another Silbermann organ). Cernay to the south was also savagely despoiled in the Great War, though parts of its mid thirteenth-century fortifications were spared. Drive west from here along the D35 to Thann on the River Thur, persevering through Vieux-Thann and the industrial zone to the main town itself and the astounding gothic church of Saint-Thiébaut, instantly recognizable from its spidery spire, soaring fretted and delicate from an elegant square tower above the multi-coloured tiled roofs of the church. As a local rhyme proclaims:

The bell-tower of Strasbourg cathedral is taller,
the steeple at Freiburg is bigger;
but ours at Thann is the loveliest.

The late fifteenth-century church at Hartmannswiller happily survived the conflict which raged here in World War I.

St Thiébaut outside his church at Thann. The sombre saint would surely have disapproved of the costly architectural riches of the interior.

The sculptures of this church are justly famous. I am especially fond of the twelve apostles carved on the north side, with St Peter (holding keys) and St Paul (holding a sword) in the middle. The entrance bears a portrait of St John the Baptist in a marvellously hairy coat, as well as another of St Thiébaut with two children. The fifteenth-century glass in the east window is stunning, like all the minor masterpieces that go to make up this great building. Search the stalls for the chubby carving of a bespectacled man. I'm sure I know him.

Napoleon's General Kléber built Thann town hall before he changed his profession from architect to soldier. Although Louis XIV decreed that the town's thirteenth-century château should be demolished, its

ruined round tower still stands, as do some of the town fortifications, including a couple of towers.

An old rhyme runs:

> From Thann in the Rangen,
> From Guebweiler in the Wannen,
> From Turkheim in the Brandt,
> Come the best wines in the land.

Here then is perhaps where you should sample the three other great wines of Alsace that were not specifically recommended by Patrick Fulgraff to accompany his New Year's Eve meal: Sylvaner, Muscat d'Alsace and Gewürztraminer. Sylvaner is fruity and light, ideal drunk with salads or on a picnic. Muscat d'Alsace is nothing like the rich yellow Muscat of the Languedoc, but is far drier and sharper. As for Gewürztraminer, produced from what is a descendant of the Traminer grape and thus sometimes dubbed Traminer-Gewürztraminer, here is a tantalizingly piquant drink.

Apart from the Champagne country, Alsace is the most northerly of the wine regions of France, and the high quality of what is produced owes much to the slopes of the Vosges to the west which shelter the vineyards from harsh winds and too much rain. Divided from the German wines of the Rheingau, the Rheinhessen and the Palatinate only by the great river itself, wines from the vineyards of Alsace are uniquely distinctive. As in Germany, the vintners offer you both those known as Spätlese (that is, pressed from grapes that have been allowed to remain on the vine longer than usual, thus producing an unusually ripe and rich wine) and the exquisite Beerenauslese wines (pressed from yet more succulent, over-ripe grapes). In Alsace these varieties are described as *vendange tardive* and *sélection de grains nobles* respectively. Re-

I find this rustic Passion scene outside Balgau, south of Neuf-Brisach, rather moving.

markably, nearly 50 per cent of the wine drunk in France today comes from Alsace – always marketed in the distinctive slender, green, flute-like bottles. By a decree of 1972, every Alsace wine must be bottled in the region where it was produced.

Grand Cru on an Alsace wine label indicates a drink with a higher alcoholic content and perhaps offering a higher quality than most. Alsatians also drink their own sparkling wine, the elegant Crémant d'Alsace, produced in both white and rosé varieties, the former from pinot blanc grapes, the latter from pinot noir. Crémant d'Alsace is made like champagne, the bottled wine placed in racks in the cellars and each day turned by hand. Alsatians drink it very cold in lovely fluted glasses at birthdays, weddings, first communions and on New Year's Day. And they mix it into cocktails.

Sleep off the wine at Thann and then take the fast N66 south-east to Mulhouse. To reach the town you cannot avoid passing the awful Tower of Europe, though its water display is some recompense, looking like a watery dandelion. Turn left into the place de la Réunion, fronted by the multi-coloured renaissance town hall. Built in 1553, it now houses the region's historical museum, so you can wander through its lovely rooms at will. In the same square is the Calvinist church of Saint-Étienne, built in 1858 but incorporating the most important fourteenth-century stained glass in Alsace, which once adorned its predecessor. I am always amazed that visitors are allowed to climb the circular stairs to the galleries and view such treasures close up. The sequence starts in the north gallery with the story of Adam and Eve, though the backs of pews conceal, for instance, much of the birth of Eve. I like the depiction of Jesus's baptism very much: he stands in the cold blue water with a little towel round his waist. Avert your eyes from the mid twentieth-century glass in the west window and climb the south gallery to explore more fourteenth-century delights – the entombment, souls in purgatory, Jesus slaying the devil, Jonah emerging from the whale (a symbol of the resurrection), Daniel in the lions' den, Samson tearing open the jaws of a lion, Jesus's resurrection, Elijah off to heaven while his successor Elisha watches.

It was on the splendid instrument in this gloomy church that the redoubtable organist Charles Münch taught the young Albert Schweitzer, and you can hear some of the Bach that the great doctor loved at the annual Bach festival each May. Mulhouse also boasts a synagogue built in 1849 in an oriental style and more museums than anyone could dream of to while away winter afternoons, a fine arts museum, a textile printing museum, a fire-fighters' museum, a wallpaper museum, a railway-train museum, a tropical aquarium (known as the oceanographic museum), a ceramic museum and France's national automobile museum. If the weather is fine, I much prefer to wander in the botanical garden. There is also a small zoo here with some 200 species of animals and birds, a few roaming freely.

It is time to head back towards the Rhine. Look for the signs pointing to *Allemagne* and take the D39 out of Mulhouse through the Forest of the Harth, turning left at Bantzenheim along the D468 to drive for 25 kilometres to Neuf-Brisach, a place which should be included in every Rhine tour. This is the last of the fortified towns built by the great military engineer Vauban, and his masterpiece. Standing only 6 kilometres from the Rhine and therefore essential for the protection of the frontiers of France, it was begun on the orders of Louis XIV in 1699 and finished in 1708. To attract citizens the king granted the town exemptions from taxes, free building land, and the right to hold fairs and markets. Vauban's defensive

---

Mulhouse town hall, built in the sixteenth century to replace the building burnt down in 1551, and decorated by the brilliant Christopher Bockstoffer and his son Lucas.

Above **Natural gold near Marckolsheim.**

Right **The secluded church outside Eschau, east of Geispolsheim on the banks of the Rhine, a village which flourished under the protection of a monastery founded in the eighth century.**

ramparts are still in remarkably fine condition – a double set of walls with a double moat. You can walk round them, pausing at the four great gates: the porte de Bâle, the porte de Belfort, the porte de Colmar and the porte du Fort Mortier. The porte de Belfort houses a fascinating museum devoted to Vauban. If you walk through the gates here and down some steps, you can take a gentle stroll around the moat.

Neuf-Brisach is a perfect classical garrison town, its streets running at right-angles to each other. The elegant church in the French classical style was designed by François Chevalier between 1731 and 1777 in collaboration with Joseph Massol, the man who was responsible for the Château de Rohan at Strasbourg. Dedicated to St Louis in flattery of the French king, the church has two baroque altars, a high altar with wooden Corinthian columns painted to simulate marble, and the much finer example dedicated to Jesus, Mary and St John in the right transept. I find it quite astonishing that this church has been entirely reconstructed after being burned to the ground on 5 February 1945. The new building was consecrated on 5 October thirty years later. For once I have no objection to the modern stained glass (by Paul and Adeline Bony), which knows its humble place and does not detract from the airy lightness of the church.

From Neuf-Brisach drive north to Geispolsheim along the D468 towards Strasbourg 70 kilometres away. The road parallels the Rhine and the Rhône-Rhine canal for much of its length, running through Marckolsheim, Artolsheim (with its charming half-timbered houses along the main street) and Diebols-heim (with a defensive moat and almost smothered in flowers in summer). The Rhine plain stretches away absolutely flat on either side, though you can see the hills of Alsace rising in the distance and the heights of the Black Forest across the river in Germany.

The attractive old fortified town of Geispolsheim is full of half-timbered, shuttered houses, with window boxes overflowing with red geraniums forming vivid patches of colour at the right time of year. Here you are in Alsatian sauerkraut country, with some 1000 tonnes of this delicacy – more accurately known as *choucroute* here – being produced annually from this area. The heart of the region is the appropriately named Krautegersheim to the south, where the German word for cabbage, *Kraut*, was added as a prefix to Egersheim in the sixteenth century. The pickled cabbage – known in Alsace patois as *Sürkrüt* or *Gumbostkrüt* – is celebrated here at a special festival at the end of September and the beginning of October, a feature of other villages such as Geispolsheim as well. A couple of these villages are worth a visit. The half-timbered houses and baroque church of lovely Blaesheim, a mere 3 kilometres away, lie picturesquely crowded together at the foot of the curious isolated hill known as the Gloeckelsberg. The romantic romanesque tower at the summit is all that remains of a church destroyed during the Thirty Years' War. Entzheim, to the north, although now dominated by Strasbourg airport, has elegant courtyarded houses surrounding an eighteenth-century church. I remember this village particularly for the magnificent displays of *tartes flambées*. These 'blazing tarts' crammed with apples, strawberries, raspberries, rhubarb, damsons, cherries and plums are a reminder that Alsace is known for its orchards and soft fruits as well as its vines, and that these are the basis of its liqueurs. Two of the most delightful to my mind are the damson liqueurs which the Alsatians call Quetsche and an unusual greengage liqueur. The most expensive is undoubtedly Houx, distilled from holly berries.

Leave Entzheim by the D392 in the direction of

The renaissance clock on the 'Metzig', Molsheim. Two angels sound the hours. Once an abattoir, the Metzig is now the local history museum, where you can trace the long history of this region.

Saint-Dié and after a kilometre or so you reach a roundabout and follow the sign for Molsheim along the N420, the start of a tour through unspoilt towns and villages of such remarkable charm that I know of no other part of France which is as beautiful. Molsheim, a delicious town still encircled by fortifications incorporating a fourteenth-century gateway, perfectly introduces them. One of the most remarkable buildings here is the abattoir in the main square, probably the only one in the world adorned with graceful gothic balconies, an ornate clock, a double staircase and gargoyles. This is the so-called 'Metzig', built by the butchers' guild in 1525 and now housing a museum of local history on the first floor. The cellar serves wine. In the square outside the lion crowning the sixteenth-century fountain carries Molsheim's coat of arms.

Take rue de l'Église from here, a twisting street lined with fine gabled houses, and turn left into rue Notre-Dame. I always pause at the insignificant metal plaque which tells you that you are passing the former Jesuit college, founded in 1580 by Bishop Jean de Manderscheid to further the Counter-Reformation, a sign of the triumph of Catholicism in mid sixteenth-century Alsace. Pope Paul V made it a Catholic university in 1617, but this was transferred to Strasbourg by Louis XIV. Yet Molsheim was once staunchly Protestant. Erasmus Guerber, who was inspired by Martin Luther to lead the peasants' revolt of 1525, was born here.

Next to the college is the church of Notre-Dame, another symbol of renewed Catholic strength, built by the flamboyant Bavarian master Christopher Wamser in 1615–17. The tower of St Michael, embellished with a couple of balconies and topped by a dome, rises from the centre of the west façade, a perfect expression of Jesuit grandeur. When Cardinal de Rohan, Bishop of Strasbourg from 1704 to 1749, paid his first visit to Molsheim church, the sophisticated prelate exclaimed, 'Nowhere else in France have I seen anything comparable.' Before you go in, seek out the carving of the scene at the Garden of Gethsemane, Jesus praying, his disciples sleeping, his enemies appearing from the rear. Inside the church the tremendous height of the nave is initially overwhelming, drawing the eye away from some excellent statuary, carvings and frescoes. The best of these include figures of the Virgin Mary standing on the moon, of Jesus holding himself as an infant in the apse and St Jerome wearing his cardinal's hat on the pulpit, his foot on a friendly lion who looks understandably miserable. The chapel of the seven sacraments in the mini-transept with its classical gable is adorned with vivid frescoes of the life of St Ignatius Loyola, founder of the Jesuits. When I last saw them in 1986 they were in rotten condition. The one to the left of the altar shows the saint after he has thrown himself into icy water, refusing to emerge from this potentially lethal situation until a young libertine on a bridge promises not to go into a brothel. Those on the opposite side, equally decrepit, portray the life of the Virgin Mary. The west window of the church is good, and I find the two modern side windows by the ubiquitous Max Ingrand less offensive than his usual work.

Apart from Ingrand's glass, the sole modern intrusions are on the north side, where two columns by a renaissance doorway sorrowfully commemorate those who fell in the wars of 1870–71, 1914–18 and 1939–45. This rather sad spot happens to be one of the best places to admire the pleasing variations in the pale pink decorated tracery.

Walk on down rue de la Monnaie to see the former mint (or Hôtel de la Monnaie) of 1573 before returning to the centre of the town. Then leave Molsheim by crossing the River Bruche and branching right on to the D35. Shortly afterwards you will reach the ancient gate of Mutzig, adorned with a painting of St George.

Typical Alsatian houses and one of the three defensive gateways at Boersch, a sign of the perils of the Middle Ages.

The château built by the prince-bishops of Strasbourg is now a brewery, a reminder that beer is almost as important as wine in Alsace and that Mutzig has been a beer town since 1812, when the Wagner family first started fermenting hops here. It is also a celebrated garrison town, still ready to defend the frontiers of France should this be necessary. Appropriately, Antoine-Alphonse Chassepot, inventor of the powerful rifle that bears his name, was born here in 1833. But there are many gentler aspects of the town too. The sound of a seventeenth-century fountain fills the main square, and I like the saracen's head carved over the clock on the sleepy town hall.

Three kilometres further along the D35 you reach Rosheim, set against a beautiful backcloth of hills. When I first came here I did not know what to expect and was amazed to be faced by a series of battlemented and fortified gates along the road, the first of which sports both a peaceful drawing of Our Lady and also slits for dropping debris on invaders. This extraordinary place has the remains of no fewer than three sets of fortifications from the thirteenth, fourteenth and fifteenth centuries. Even so, the whole village was slaughtered in 1622 by soldiers of the Count of Mansfield. You cannot miss the church of St Peter and St Paul on your right as you enter the town, a romanesque marvel, with a crucifix dated 1795 set outside it. Legend has it that angels with flaming torches drove back Mansfield's pillaging soldiers and prevented them from destroying the building. Before you go inside, explore the external carvings. I like the contrast between the unfortunate man captured by four dragons and the happier figure at the foot of the octagonal tower, a goblet in his hand (rightly, since Rosheim lies on the Alsace wine route). The west door is delicately beautiful. So is the north door. The five-sided apse is both simple and complex, chiselled with heavenly romanesque symbols of the four evangelists. In order to get inside you have to obtain the key from the *pâtisserie* opposite, for which the proprietor

reasonably enough expects a small fee, but I would urge anyone not to miss an opportunity to see the mix of gothic and romanesque pillars and capitals, each one inventively different. There is also another Silbermann organ. Then you can relax with a picnic on the grass outside, or else buy a delicacy from the *pâtisserie* as I did when you take the key back.

The massive classical church of Saint-Étienne 500 metres up the main street is also interesting in that Salins de Montfort designed it to incorporate the late twelfth-century romanesque belfry of an older church. Close by stands the oldest house in Alsace, a surprisingly tall building dating from around 1170.

At the end of the village, turn left down the D35 and drive 3 kilometres to quiet, sleepy Boersch, another fortified wine village with a group of superb half-timbered houses, a renaissance town hall and a well sporting six buckets – all in the place de l'Hôtel de Ville. This little square is shadowed by the romanesque bell-tower of the church of Saint-Médard, which is notable for its twelfth-century frescoes, only seen by peering through the grill when the church is locked. At the cool *Winstub* opposite you have a choice of Sylvaner, Riesling or the humble Edelzwicker. Before leaving Boersch stand for a moment or two in the main square listening to the sound of running water from the streams flowing underground here, controlled by a lock above the village.

Now follow the D35 for 2 kilometres to Ottrott, where you should seek out the twelfth-century church of Saint-Nicolas, with an outside staircase leading up to its gallery. Only the apse of the romanesque building remains, for in 1622 during the Thirty Years' War the nave and the rest of the village were burned down. The main parish church, filled with baroque furnishings

---

An Alsatian delicacy for sale at Barr, a wine town beautifully situated at the foot of the Vosges mountains.

and a Silbermann organ, was built in 1771. If you come here between July and September on a Sunday or a public holiday, you can take a ride to Rosheim and back in an old railway carriage pulled by a locomotive built in 1906.

The village of Ottrott lies 3 kilometres west of Obernai, an Alsatian town with everything you have come to expect of them, plus a bit more. Surrounded by terraced vineyards, protected by double ramparts studded with no fewer than twenty towers (built in the thirteenth and sixteenth centuries), filled with stone and half-timbered medieval and renaissance houses, this is a town of squares and narrow streets, of picturesque corners and delightful details. The local tourist office is pleasingly housed in the oldest building, the 72-metre high Kappelturm, once the belfry of a church, its gaunt lower parts built in 1285, its fanciful upper stages in 1597. The tiny ruelle des Juifs opposite is entrancing.

Odile, the seventh-century patron saint of Alsace, is said to have been born in a house just behind this information office. Although the saint came into the world blind, she miraculously recovered her sight when she was baptised. Her statue stands on a fountain in the place du Marché, between the sixteenth-century cornmarket (dated 1554 over the balcony) and the half gothic, half renaissance town hall, with an oriel window and balcony.

To see the castellated ruins of the former château, walk down rue du Marché from here, along rue du Général-Gouraud and right into rue du Château. Or stroll down rue du Chanoine-Gryss from the place du Marché past a fifteenth-century well with six buckets to see the parish church, whose slender twin towers dominate the town. The statue in front of the church commemorates Monsignor Charles-Émile Freppel, Bishop of Tours, whose heart is in an urn inside. This saintly and patriotic man, who died at Angers in 1891 at a time when Alsace was in German hands, loved Obernai, his birthplace; but he laid down certain conditions for allowing his heart back home. His will declared, 'I desire my heart to be taken to the parish church of Obernai only when Alsace has once more become French.'

Astonishingly, the church which houses his heart actually straddles the River Ehn. How does it stay intact? One crack on the south side of the building runs from top to bottom. But what a fine decorated apse there is inside, filled with fifteenth-century stained glass. It is said that Grünewald himself designed some of the St Sebastian window to the left of the altar of the Holy Sepulchre. A great nineteenth-century chandelier hangs from the Byzantine-style dome. Alas, you can no longer see the statue of the Madonna of Obernai, which once graced this building, as she was stolen in 1975, appropriately enough on the feast of the Assumption. A picture of the statue marks the place where she stood.

Going south from Obernai along the N422 look for the turning right to Barr, a wine town delightfully situated amidst vineyards at the foot of the Vosges. Winding streets with overhanging buildings, a paved square full of half-timbered houses and a town hall with a courtyard boasting a double staircase and colonnades create an exquisitely typical Alsace gem. In summer Barr is not surprisingly filled with tourists, and has responded to this influx by hosting two major wine festivals in July and on the second Sunday of October.

The vineyard-lined route to Sélestat to the south passes through Mittelbergheim, which dubs itself 'one of the most beautiful villages of France' and where notices declare that 'Here wine is king'. After the lovely village of Andlau, where you can see the square keep and polygonal defensive walls of the ruined

The gothic parish church of St Sebastian at Dambach-la-Ville on the way to Sélestat from Barr has an exquisite baroque high altar.

Above Heavenly protection for the harvest outside Sélestat, a testament to the fecundity of rural Alsace.

Right The River Ill near Sélestat, whose delightful narrow streets were a haven for sixteenth-century humanists.

78

Left A double ring of fortifications guards Bergheim and the church of Our Lady, notable for its powerful bell-tower and gothic apse.

Above A massive defensive gateway at Riquewihr, a remarkably unspoilt survival from the sixteenth and seventeenth centuries.

81

château de Spesbourg, make a small detour east to Epfig along the D603, following winding roads through more vineyards. At a T-junction in the village the sign for the chapel of Sainte-Marguerite suddenly appears on the corner.

This bizarre treat is not for the faint-hearted, for the cemetery chapel of Sainte-Marguerite is also a grisly ossuary. Hundreds and hundreds of grinning skulls are neatly arranged on top of each other in a sort of wire cage, balanced by the occasional arm or leg bone. Thankfully, they are just out of reach, or I suppose many people would not be able to resist reaching in and patting the skulls on their dead heads. If you feel like a prayer inside the cemetery chapel, where God the Father blesses us from a fresco in the apse, you must get the key from house no. 270 outside the gates. Personally I felt the dust between my teeth and needed a drink.

The N422 now runs directly to the fortified town of Sélestat, the home of Alsatian humanists on the eve of the Reformation, two of whom, the celebrated Beatus Rhenanus and the Protestant reformer Martin Bucer, were born here. Rhenanus left the town his magnificent library, now housed in the cornmarket. On a gentler note, it is well worth walking round the ramparts for glorious views over the lovely Alsatian countryside to the Vosges. In the middle distance is the lowering shape of medieval Haut-Koenigsbourg, a massive defensive château restored on the personal orders of Kaiser Bill. To the south and east stretches the Illwald forest, now a nature reserve. From wherever you are walking you will see two great churches in Sélestat itself, the austere sandstone and granite Sainte-Foy and the fourteenth-century Saint-Georges, with a 60-metre tower and magical stained glass.

A forest of vine posts for succulent Alsatian grapes outside Riquewihr.

You get a closer view of Haut-Koenigsbourg on the road from Sélestat to Ribeauvillé. This route passes close to the wine village of Bergheim with its old shady squares and fortified gateway, where those houses selling the local vintages have maps of the vineyards on their walls and lists of the prizes their wines have won. Ribeauvillé itself is as lovely as anywhere I have seen in Alsace, with streets again flanked by overhanging timber-framed houses. I particularly like the friendly lion that crouches on the column of the fountain. On the first Sunday in September, known as the minstrels' feast, this fountain is adapted to dispense free wine rather than water. The Fiddlers' King strolls through the town leading a procession of floats and citizens decked out in medieval costume.

From here the D1B takes you to fortified Riquewihr, the town where the vintners of Alsace met in the sixteenth century and agreed to produce only seven main varieties of wine. Resplendent with geraniums in summer, Riquewihr is an unbelievable survival from the Middle Ages, with most of its buildings predating the Thirty Years' War. The upper storeys of delightfully crooked houses often overhang the narrow streets so far that they almost touch each other. Everywhere there are representations of the coat of arms of the house of Württemberg, which took over Riquewihr in 1324. I feel the proud lords would not be happy to see their château turned into a post-office museum.

Some of the finest Alsatian grapes are grown on the sunny slopes of the Schoeneberg and the Sporen outside Riquewihr. Perhaps the composer of this celebrated Alsatian dialect rhyme was thinking of them when he wrote his verse:

If you must drink water, be sure to wrap up well;
Water can freeze your stomach as you eat.
Best of all, I counsel you to set it to one side;
Drink in moderation our old and subtle wine.

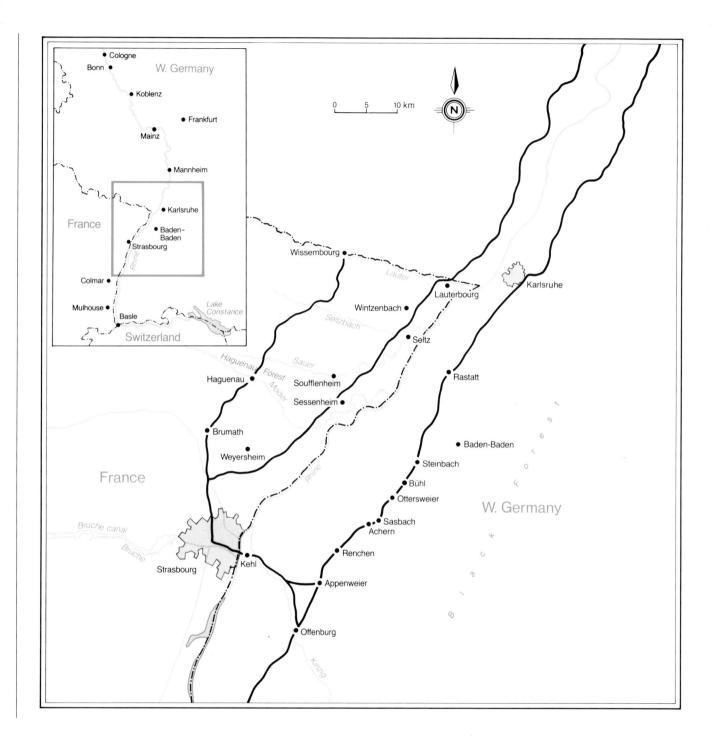

3
At the Heart of Europe

Strasbourg – Appenweier – Achern – Baden-Baden –
Seltz – Lauterbourg – Wissembourg – Haguenau –
Soufflenheim – Brumath

The stretch of the Rhine between Germany and Alsace has been disputed for centuries, passing from one fierce ruler to another from the time of the Celts and Romans virtually up to the present day. Though countless humble men and women have suffered at the hands of the warlike and greedy, and most of the towns and villages along the river have been pillaged or put to the torch during their history, this region has also benefited from the cultures of those who have governed it, resulting in a rich mix of art and architecture.

Strasbourg – literally 'the city of the routes' – is the undisputed centre of this region, standing at the point where the trade route from northern Europe to Italy crossed the Rhine, as well as prominently positioned on the great river itself. The truth of General de Gaulle's remark that the Rhine is not a river but a road is seen nowhere better than here, the fourth largest port in France. Strasbourg is a crossroads in other senses as well, for centuries acting as an intellectual, spiritual and political melting pot. Its significance was recognized when the city was chosen in 1969 as the capital of Europe, the permanent forum of the assembly of the Council of Europe, the home of the European parliament and the seat of the European court of human rights. It is by far the largest and most complex city in Alsace.

A good place to start exploring Strasbourg is the huge place Kléber, named after Napoleon's General J.-B. Kléber who was born in this city in 1753 and assassinated in Cairo in 1800. Before his time great military parades were held here and the square was known as the place d'Armes. When Kléber's ashes were reverently brought back from Cairo, to be placed under the posthumous statue sculpted by Philippe Grass, the city re-dedicated the square to him. Now he stands flanked by reliefs commemorating two of his great battles – the victory at Altenkirchen in 1796 and the battle of Heliopolis, fought on 12 March 1800. Behind Kléber's effigy sits a sphinx, and the statue is inscribed with one of his celebrated calls to arms: 'Soldiers! One responds to insult only by victories. Prepare for battle.'

Kléber looks across the square at a delightful group of higgledy-piggledy houses, all in different styles. On his left stands the pink classical opera house, ornamented with busts of Schubert, Rossini, Beethoven, Haydn and a number of lesser composers. To remind us of the traumatic history of the twentieth century, a plaque on the wall declares Strasbourg's solidarity with the Polish freedom movement:

Solidarinosc Vivra
13.12.81 – 13.12.82

Another side of the square is dominated by the vast Aubette, built in the eighteenth century as the city barracks. The name Aubette derives from the French word for dawn, *aube*, when reveille sounded and the soldiers reluctantly rose from their beds.

The façade of this building was decorated in the first half of the twentieth century by Jean Arp, who was born here in 1887, and his wife Sophie. Arp first trained as an artist in Strasbourg, but after a short spell in Paris he was soon in Munich as a leading member of the avant-garde *Blaue Reiter* school, before returning to Paris and befriending Picasso and Modigliani. Taking refuge in Zurich during World War I, Arp and his wife took up surrealism and abstract art. Just as he himself had suffered in World War I, so his art was to suffer during World War II, for the Nazis who occupied Strasbourg decided the decorations on the Aubette were decadent and destroyed them.

Hitler's soldiers also disliked the honour paid to a French military hero in this square, removed Kléber's statue and buried his remains elsewhere. When the war was over the citizens of Strasbourg brought them back. The general's birthplace is only a stone's throw from here across the place de l'Homme-de-Fer – named after the life-size model of a soldier dressed in sixteenth-century armour over what is now a pharmacist's shop but which used to be a gunsmith's – and down rue du Fossé-des-Tanneurs, where it is no. 18.

The general's statue does not look towards his birthplace but towards the opposite corner of the square and the rue des Grandes-Arcades, a fine arcaded street which includes a sweet classical building dated 1801 that is surmounted by a statue of Aesculepius, the Greek god of medicine. The end of this street debouches into another square dedicated to a Strasbourg hero, the tree-shaded place Gutenberg. Although there is one monumental late sixteenth-century building here – once the town hall but now housing the chamber of commerce and the city information office – this is a much gentler spot than the domineering place Kléber. Even the renaissance chamber of commerce manages to remain graceful while asserting its proper importance, with a façade on which Tuscan motifs for the first floor have been skilfully combined with Ionic for the second and Corinthian for the third. Arcades lead through the vaulted ground floor. The main doorway is ornamented with a bust of Hermes and a couple of lions, and the high tiled roof is pierced with graceful dormer windows.

Gutenberg's statue in the middle of the *place* commemorates the fact that it was while living in Strasbourg in the first half of the fifteenth century that he devised his revolutionary printing-press. It brought him little gain. The brilliant inventor was frequently reduced to borrowing money from friends and in November 1442 gleaned a large loan from the chapter of St Thomas's church here (on the security of his friend Martin Brechter), which he never managed to repay in full. Although the church registers do show that Gutenberg met the annual interest on the loan each November until 1456, he failed to meet his dues the following year. The chapter went to considerable expense to have both him and Martin Brechter arrested. The two men eventually paid up, but that was the last time the clergy saw the colour of their money. From November 1458 the church registers reveal annual attempts to have the two men arrested in a vain attempt to get back the loan. The arrears and the expenses incurred by the clergy of St Thomas in pursuit of Gutenberg and his defaulting

Waterways and graceful bridges enhance Strasbourg's charm.

colleague are recorded each year until 1474, when the chapter must have realized that the great printer had been dead for six years.

In spite of this peccadillo, on the next three centenaries of Gutenberg's death Strasbourg celebrated his invention with great pride. In 1840 they went further and commissioned the distinguished sculptor David d'Angers to design the statue that now stands among the trees of the *place*. Gutenberg holds a scroll inscribed with the Biblical words 'And there was light' (*Et la lumière fut*). Reliefs around the plinth of the monument attribute virtually every subsequent human achievement after the invention of printing to Gutenberg's genius, depicting other great benefactors of humanity who used his invention to inspire the world. These illustrious figures include Mozart, those men of science Copernicus and Newton, the brilliant mathematician Fermat, great artists such as Raphael and Albrecht Dürer, German men of letters of the calibre of Goethe, Klopstock and Schiller, the poet Milton (his blind eyes closed) and philosophers such as Spinoza, Confucius and Rousseau. The great Benjamin Franklin and George Washington are here, as well as Lafayette, the friend of independent America. The English philanthropist William Wilberforce is also among them, freeing little slaves, his left arm lying on a printing-press, his right arm cuddling a naked curly-haired black baby, while in the square today black Tunisians offer trinkets for sale.

One of Strasbourg's most illustrious citizens who took advantage of Gutenberg's invention was born the son of an innkeeper in 1457. Sebastian Brant, author of the famous *The Ship of Fools*, taught ecclesiastical and Roman law at the University of Basle, where he had been an outstanding student. He returned to Strasbourg and in 1503 became the city clerk, nine years after writing his much admired, endlessly reprinted, much plagiarized masterpiece *Das Narrenschiff*. It is the story of 112 fools on board a ship that, they vainly hope, will bring them by way of Utopia to the Fools' Paradise. On their voyage they are shipwrecked and everyone perishes. Brant casts his net widely, castigating alike dunces, libertines, corrupt clergy, bad parents, superstitious idiots and those unable to take a joke. His first fool is a collector of useless books. In Edwin Zeydel's charming translation, the man announces himself:

> Of splendid books I own no end,
> But few that I can comprehend.

Fool number five is the old fool, lamenting that he can no longer behave so foolishly as of yore:

> Clear water I have turned to slime
> And practised evil every time.
> That I'm no longer quite as bad
> As once I was, that makes me sad.

The old fool takes comfort from the fact that he can teach his son to behave as stupidly as he himself once did.

This was the eve of the Reformation, and although Sebastian Brant remained a firm Catholic, he did not hesitate to attack unworthy clergy:

> Another type I'd have you mark
> That on the fools' ship should embark
> Has recently been much increased,
> For every peasant wants a priest
> Among his clan, to dodge and shirk
> And play the lord, but never work;
> It's not done out of veneration
> Or for the sake of soul's salvation.
> They want a high-placed relative
> On whom the other kin may live.

Though built as a pastiche of medieval gothic, St Paul's church on the River Ill, Strasbourg, is an authentically nineteenth-century romantic folly, at once beautiful and gloomy.

Such clergymen, Brant alleged, saw no need for scholarship; all they desired were benefices.

The Ship of Fools was brilliantly illustrated with satirical woodcuts depicting each fool. Soon others in Strasbourg who did not share Brant's devotion to the Holy See would take up his criticisms of incompetent and venal clergy. Humanists such as the learned Beatus Rhenanus and the German patriot Jakob Wimpheling poured out tracts printed by Gutenberg's techniques which brought new learning to Christendom and undermined the old order.

As for the leading Protestant Reformers themselves, John Calvin lived for a time here. Here too the Dominican monk Martin Bucer renounced his vows, married a former nun, and propagated the Reformation. The priest Matthias Zell, son of a vintner of Kaysersberg, was excommunicated for preaching Lutheranism in Strasbourg. He too took a wife and a year later in 1524 took the bold step of celebrating the Mass in German, not in Latin. A Protestant university was set up, and the cathedral itself became for a time Protestant. Its Catholic bishops were exiled until Louis XIV of France became suzerain of the city in 1681.

On a Saturday in May 1986 I sat in the sun outside the café 'Au Gutenberg', brooding on such matters and eating snail soup and warm onion tart washed down with a glass of beer. Known as *tarte à l'oignon* elsewhere in France, onion tarts are called *Zwiebelkuchen* in this part of Alsace. It was a typically Alsatian meal in splendid surroundings, part French, part German, but quintessentially its own self. Although escargots often appear in soup in Alsace, they are usually served as *escargots à l'Alsacienne*, cooked in garlic butter. Normally this delicacy would be accompanied with wine – a white Riesling or a Sylvaner – but on that day I thought beer would be more suitable. This Alsatian beverage has been drunk in Strasbourg for centuries and you can still see the little ruelle de la Bière where it was first sold in 1259.

Perhaps fortified with a meal, leave place Gutenberg

for the cathedral by way of the pedestrianized rue des Hallebardes. As a foretaste of what is to come, almost immediately a fretted spire appears above the rooftops, its bells hanging in an open belfry in descending order of size. A notice just before you turn right into the place de la Cathédrale tells you that the rue des Hallebardes was once the Roman Via Praetoria. The Austrians later called it Spiessgasse, and then the French renamed it rue des Tartines in 1765. Off to the left runs the rue des Orfèvres, once the street of the goldsmiths (and formerly known as Goldschmidt-gasse).

One superb building, covered in painted carvings, stands out from the picturesque houses which line the rue des Hallebardes, their upper storeys overhanging the street. This is the Maison Kammerzell on the corner of the cathedral square, prosaically named after a grocer who sold it to the cathedral chapter in 1879. Its ground floor is built of stone and dates from the fifteenth century, but the exotic building above was commissioned in the 1580s by a merchant who had it embellished with carvings depicting the five senses, the signs of the zodiac, mythological heroes, medieval legends and the seven ages of man. The Maison Kammerzell is now a restaurant, fittingly decorated with an entertaining fresco by Leo Schnugg illustrating a huge tureen of soup that was brought here by ship from Zurich in 1576. Legend has it that the soup was still warm after a voyage lasting 17 hours.

Opposite rises the cathedral, its west front encased in a fretwork of stone that seems to have been woven, its great rose window gleaming, its octagonal tower with four staircase turrets tapering to a slender spiky spire. Long ago the Romans built a temple to Mars on this spot. In the sixth century Christians replaced it with a chapel dedicated to the Virgin Mary, and Our Lady is still worshipped in the cathedral of Notre-Dame. After an earlier church was burnt down by marauding Swedes in the first years of the eleventh century, Bishop Wernher von Habsburg started to

Chubby cherubs on Strasbourg cathedral, some of the legendary carvings on this great building.

build the present romanesque core of the cathedral in 1015. His building was frequently damaged by fire, for most of its inner structures were made of wood. Finally Bishop Konrad of Hüneburg set in motion the rebuilding of the east end in 1176, enlarging the apse and crossing. The heart of Strasbourg cathedral is thus a late romanesque masterpiece, built just at the time when gothic architecture was beginning to infiltrate Germany.

Erwin von Steinbach, a gothic architect of legendary skill, took over as cathedral architect in 1284, seven years after work had begun on covering the west façade with its intricate decoration and beautiful sculptures, with niches housing statues of kings and emperors. His work was completed by his son Jean,

who succeeded him in 1318. Theirs is the rose window, 7 metres wide and modelled on that at Chartres. Erwin and his son planned to finish the west end of the cathedral with two bell-towers rising over the doorways to left and right. The wall pierced by two huge twin windows which now joins the towers was a radical change in plan made after their deaths.

By 1365 all was finished, save for the single spire which rises 142 metres above the ground. I find it hard to believe that this is the work of three men, so unified is the total effect. The first stage was the responsibility of the Freiburg architect Michael Parler, who built the bell-tower in 1384; 15 years later Ulrich von Benjamin, architect of Ulm cathedral, began the octagon above Michael Parler's tower; and in 1419 the Cologne architect Johannes Hütz began work on the spiky eight-sided pyramid which crowns the whole edifice and was finished in 1439. 'Sublime' was Goethe's word for the whole effect, and he was right. 'How often I returned to view its dignity and magnificence from every side, from every distance, at every time of the day', he remembered. 'Blissful, I developed inside me the power to understand as well as enjoy it.'

In 1770 the sight of the cathedral had transformed the young Johann Wolfgang Goethe's typically eighteenth-century distaste for gothic architecture into entranced rapture. Goethe himself tells the story. He had come to Strasbourg as a student, his head, he admitted, filled with general notions of good taste, based not on making his own judgments but on what he had heard from others. 'I praised harmony and purity of form, and was a sworn enemy of the arbitrary confusion of the gothic,' he confessed. Gothic meant for him indefinite, disorganized, unnatural, overladen. In Strasbourg cathedral he expected to find 'a misshapen grotesque monster'.

Standing before the great edifice he was instantly converted, overwhelmed with emotion. It seemed to him almost as if its long-dead architect, Erwin von Steinbach, was talking to him. 'Why are you

Biblical stories in stone: the central porch at the west end of Strasbourg cathedral (*above*) is crowded with illustrations of Biblical epics (*left*) for the edification of devout, illiterate medieval Christians. The story of Adam and Eve is at top right.

astonished?' Erwin seemed to whisper. 'All these different masses were necessary. I simply elevated arbitrary vastness to harmony.' When Goethe awoke the next morning he went immediately to his window to look out on to the cathedral. 'How fresh was its radiance in the shimmer of the misty morning light! How contentedly I stretched out my arms towards it, looking at the huge harmonious masses brought to life by countless parts!' Every component part, he decided, from the smallest to the greatest, beautifully

93

served the whole. 'How lightly this immense building soars into the air', he exclaimed. 'Everything is like filigree, made for eternity.'

An inability to see the merits of Strasbourg cathedral did not disappear with Goethe's conversion. Even Sacheverell Sitwell, a noted connoisseur of the gothic, perversely objected to sandstone cathedrals as seemingly 'cast in rusty iron'; yet he was obliged to admit that 'it is among the moments of architectural experience when one turns the corner into the narrow rue Mercière with its postcard stalls and magpie houses and sees the huge west front of Strasbourg cathedral filling the street and towering above the house roofs; and another great storey rises above that, and then the one gigantic tower.'

I am not certain that I fully understand why the west façade of Strasbourg cathedral is so overwhelmingly beautiful. Perhaps it is the combination of grand design and detailed masterpieces – the sculpted Last Judgment, the intricately worked Biblical scenes and the charming carvings of the seasons of the year. The cathedral is just as astonishing inside. Since the gothic architects who worked on the interior followed the lines of the old romanesque church, this soaring building is much wider than any of the other gothic masterpieces of northern France. The medieval stained glass is breathtaking. Old and New Testament scenes, portraits of saints, devils, emperors and martyrs, nearly all of them glazed in either the thirteenth or fourteenth centuries, flood the cathedral with colour. And for once a masterly rose window, here restored in 1845, is not obscured by an organ-case. Not that the organ should be ignored. Set at the entrance to the nave, its richly-carved case first built in 1385 was greatly elaborated five centuries later by the master organ-builder Andreas Silbermann, who incorporated some priceless earlier pipes by the fifteenth-century master Friedrich Krebs.

Superb carving in stone rather than wood adorns the pulpit half-way down the nave, sculpted with crockets, statuettes and the scene of Jesus's crucifixion, and looking for all the world like a piece of filigree jewellery. This masterpiece was designed by Hans Hammer in 1485 for the celebrated Strasbourg preacher Geiler von Kaysersberg, who was feared for his scornful denunciations of the vices of the age. Hans Hammer was obviously not without humour, for at the foot of the pulpit he carved Geiler's pet dog, sleeping through one of his master's diatribes.

A more unusual masterpiece among the many adorning the cathedral is the Angels' Pillar, often called the pillar of the Last Judgment. Three groups of delicately carved statues, dating from around 1220, fill the pillar from top to bottom. At the top Jesus is flanked by angels carrying the instruments of his passion. Then come four angels blowing their trumpets at Doomsday, and below them the four evangelists, each one identified by the symbol on which he stands: an eagle, a winged lion, a bull and an angel.

Close by is the cathedral's most cherished showpiece, the astronomical clock, a comical masterpiece that the cathedral chapter installed here in 1547 in place of an earlier instrument. By means of ingenious mechanisms this clock indicates not only the movements of the planets but also the rising and setting of the sun and the moon and religious feast days. Tobie Stimmer, who painted the renaissance case of the clock, also designed the entertaining wooden figures that come into play on the hour and on the quarter hours. Death strikes the hours, but Jesus appears and drives him away. Quarter hours are rung on bells by figures representing the four ages of man. There are models of the four seasons and the twelve apostles, and little chariots symbolize the days of the week. At 12.30 pm each day the twelve apostles pass in

---

Woven sandstone and the great rose window of Strasbourg cathedral, a stained-glass flower as fine as any in Europe.

The cathedral clock, Strasbourg, hints at the famous astronomical clock inside, tempting visitors to explore more of this red sandstone ecclesiastical masterpiece.

front of Jesus, bowing to him while he blesses them and a cock crows. Then Jesus blesses all those who are watching below.

Lastly, look out for two sixteenth-century altar triptychs glistening in gold leaf which flank the stairs to the choir. In the one dedicated to St Catherine, St Pancras and St Nicholas (who, as patron saint of pawnbrokers, carries three golden balls), the splendidly clad saints have taken over the centre of the stage, relegating the infant Jesus to the panels to left and right. One of these shows the Magi bringing him gifts, with the baby delightfully depicted with his hand in their box of gold, like some wicked shop assistant surreptitiously stealing from the till.

Ultimately of course Strasbourg cathedral is not a gallery of religious art but a house of worship, where I once attended Mass on the feast of All Saints. The service was both informal and impressive, and the church was packed for the occasion. At the free-standing altar the priests needed only to murmur into microphones for their words to be heard by the whole congregation. Bells ringing at the moment of consecration and anthems performed by the choir added to the mystical atmosphere. The communion was brought to the congregation by many priests at several points in the cathedral, each flanked by an acolyte holding a candle. Six candles lit the high altar and many more flickered in holders set into each of the pillars. There was a hint of incense.

Less mysterious than the Holy Eucharist but still thrilling are the *son-et-lumière* performances held in the nave of the cathedral from mid April until the end of September. Lights, stereophonic music and recorded commentaries are used to evoke twenty centuries of Strasbourg's history, as well as retelling the story of the cathedral itself, and recounting the many disasters from which it has emerged so triumphantly. The marauding troops and raging fires of the Middle Ages were followed by wanton despoliation at the Reformation, when men and women deliberately defaced altars and statues, believing them to be superstitious. The Revolutionaries would have pulled down the cathedral spire itself, had not a quick-witted citizen proposed that it should be adorned with a sculpted Revolutionary's bonnet instead. Even so, on the orders of the fanatical Saint-Just, nearly 300 precious statues were either mutilated or totally smashed, and the city's anguished clerk of works managed to save only 67.

The next two centuries witnessed the destructiveness of German might. On 14 July 1870 Napoleon III foolishly declared war against Prussia, an action which led to the collapse of his empire. Strasbourg heroically resisted the German assault for 45 days. On the night of

25 August the city was pitilessly bombarded, its venerable cathedral spire damaged and 1200 panels of stained glass destroyed. Other churches suffered even more. An old man skilled in the art of making stained glass recalled standing helplessly while Hans Wild's wonderful panels in the church of St Mary Magdalen melted and ran down to the ground, victims of a great fire raging within.

The Germans who conquered the city were happily not architectural vandals, and they appointed the extremely intelligent Gustav Klotz to restore the damage to the cathedral. His major gift to the great building is the octagonal tower over the crossing which he built in the romanesque style between 1877 and 1880, replacing the pseudo-gothic tower set there by J.-F. Blondel after a fire on 27 July 1759. Ironically, after Hitler's planes had bombed the city in 1944 much of Klotz's tower lay ruined and needed restoration in its turn.

If you still have enough energy after exploring the cathedral, climb the 330 steps which lead up to a platform 66 metres above the ground for a closer look at the marvellous spire and a panorama over the city. This scene inspired Roger Pilkington (in his delightful *Small Boat to Alsace*) to write, 'If there is one thing in particular which at the first glimpse distinguishes Strasbourg from other great cities, it is the row upon row of dormer windows which crowd every slope of mottled tiles, as though the Alsatians are unwilling to leave an inch of roof space or gable unused. From the top of the cathedral tower the visitor can have an astonishing view over these myriad little openings, and if he has keen eyes he can also scan the roof-tops for the patches of white which mark the whereabouts of a family of storks.' I too have repeatedly relished this bird's eye view of Strasbourg's streets and squares, with cresting waves of exquisitely tiled mansard roofs. Look north of the cathedral across its flying buttresses where the pedestrianized rue du Dôme stretches in the direction of the church of St

The Château de Rohan overlooking the river at Strasbourg, its classical columns reflecting the arrogance and self-importance of the eighteenth-century prince-bishops who built it.

Peter the Younger. Organ buffs will seek out a Silbermann masterpiece of 1770 here, well restored in our own time. The rue du Dôme itself is truly schizophrenic, half German and half French, with notices pointing you both to *Allemagne* and to *Deutschland*.

Those who do not want to explore St Peter the Younger should walk not north but south of the cathedral to find one of the greatest châteaux in all France, built in the early eighteenth century for Armand-Gaston de Rohan-Soubise, who was not only a prince of the Holy Roman Empire and landgrave of Lower Alsace but also bishop of Strasbourg. The Rohan family in fact occupied this bishopric as if it were their personal possession for most of the eighteenth century. Bishop Armand-Gaston commissioned the Parisian architect Robert de Cotte to create a palace whose north pavilions and great doorway faced the place du Château and whose main façade with its massive Corinthian columns fronted the River Ill. Today his château is a museum of fine arts, decorative arts and archaeology. The exhibits are fascinating, including splendid porcelain and works by El Greco, Rubens, Van Dyck and Goya as well as by French masters such as Greuze, Fragonard, Delacroix and Courbet; but the main purpose of any visit should be simply to view the sumptuous apartments. The royal chamber and the assembly rooms, ornamented with splendidly carved furnishings, vie with Versailles in baroque exuberance. The little apartments, the rooms lived in by the family, are rococo gems, decorated with copies of works by Nicolas Poussin and portraits of the Rohan family.

In the same square, the place du Château, are three other fine buildings, all a complete contrast to each other and to the château itself: the former Jesuit college built by Joseph Massol in 1757, a gabled house of 1347 and another built in the late sixteenth century. The courtyard of the second house has a staircase tower which is one of the most exquisite in Strasbourg.

West of the Château de Rohan is one of those charming squares that so easily evoke elegant urban life in seventeenth- and eighteenth-century Strasbourg: the place Marché-aux-Cochons-de-Lait, named after the piglets that were once sold here. Today the square is a delight of half-timbered houses with overhanging upper floors. Walking further along the river will bring you to a sixteenth-century building which used to be the city slaughterhouse and is now the history museum, and then to the delightful cour du Corbeau (crow's courtyard), surrounded with what were fishermen's lodgings. The charming wooden balconies and covered galleries here were all treated in the seventeenth century with a coat of ox blood from the nearby slaughterhouse to preserve them for ever. So too were the external staircase and the octagonal turret.

After a tour of the cathedral I hesitate to recommend another church, but if you continue along quai St-Thomas from here past the former sixteenth-century customs house you reach what is known as the Protestant cathedral, a splendid half romanesque, half gothic feast started in 1196 and finished in the fourteenth century. The most fascinating feature of this church is not the great rose window which rivals that of the cathedral itself, but the tomb placed inside at the request of the Catholic sovereign Louis XV, the last resting-place of his loyal servant Marshal Saxe. Albeit a hero, Saxe was illegitimate; he was also a Protestant, so there could be no place for his mausoleum in Catholic Saint-Denis, Paris. The Lutherans of Strasbourg proved more accommodating. By 1775 Jean-Baptiste Pigalle had finished a superb tomb for Saxe's remains, depicting the marshal, baton in hand, stepping down into his coffin which shrouded death is attempting to open, fended off by the figure of France herself. Hercules stands in attendance, overwhelmed with grief, while above him the Dutch lion, the Austrian eagle and the British leopard sit astride their broken battle standards.

If it is time to eat again there is nowhere better to do so than in the water-washed district of Strasbourg known as La Petite France, named in the eighteenth century after the French troops of the Holy Roman Emperor Francis I, who made it their favourite rendezvous when not on duty. Once the home of tanners, fishermen and millers, La Petite France is today given over to tourism, though the whole quarter

The powerful half gothic, half romanesque church of St Thomas, known as the Protestant cathedral, rises above Strasbourg's elegant streets.

remains utterly unspoilt, its gabled, galleried half-timbered houses, often with intricately carved corbels, strung along winding streets, bedecked with flowers in summer and romantically wreathed in mist in winter. Prices in the restaurants tend to go up in summer, but even then the food is by no means expensive. The finest street is probably the rue du Bain-aux-Plantes and undoubtedly the most famous restaurant is no. 42, the Maison des Tanneurs, where you can eat traditional Alsatian cuisine by the side of the Ill. A particular attraction of this area are the so-called Ponts Couverts across the river. They are no longer covered, and indeed the original medieval bridges after which they are called have long been replaced. But they are still protected by three medieval defensive towers, known as the hangman's tower, the French tower and the tower of the chains.

One of the most relaxing ways of seeing Strasbourg is to take the minibus which leaves from the cathedral and tours the old quarters of the city in the summer. During the same season pleasure boats sail from a point near the Château de Rohan for excursions along the Ill and into the Rhine itself. If you have time for a longer exploration of the city, drive across the pont du Théâtre to the monumental place de la République, a huge square created by the Germans after they annexed Alsace at the end of the Franco-Prussian war. German architects gave the city the mighty imperial palace (now called the palais du Rhin), designed by Hermann Heggert in 1883, and the grandiloquent new university library, which flank the square. Down the allée de la Robertsau from here you can see the palace of the Council of Europe, whose delegates have the

---

The colourful inns and waterside houses of La Petite France, Strasbourg, a quarter named after the soldiers of Revolutionary France, who came here to forget the horrors of military life in the late eighteenth century.

misfortune of sitting under an immense transparent dome. I should think they escape with relief between sessions to wander in the park known as the Orangerie which Le Nôtre created close by.

Leave the capital of Alsace by crossing the Rhine into Germany at the pont de l'Europe and continue east over the motorway for 15 kilometres or so to Appenweier. This apparently unexceptional place, with its pretty houses, hotels and occasional *Gasthaus*, is the unlikely setting for a magnificent baroque and rococo church with an onion dome, dedicated to St Michael. This echo of Bavarian architecture at its most riotous was built in the mid eighteenth century to plans by Franz Ignaz Ritter, who had learned his art in Würzburg. The ornate interior with a complex marble pulpit by Johannes Schütz has been sumptuously restored. Angels fly up and down the canopy of the high altar, looking down on the statues of St Sebastian pierced with three golden arrows and St Wendelin which flank it on either side. A painting by J. Plummer depicting the church's patron flinging Lucifer and his angels out of heaven is outclassed, in my view, by the late gothic panel of the Madonna presenting the infant Jesus to his grandmother, St Anne. Our Lady wears a golden crown and St Anne is giving her divine grandson a pomegranate. The church is about 50 metres from the station in Appenweier down a road to the left, and is easily identified from the painting of St Michael with a blazing sword opposite the entrance.

Returning to the centre of the village, where a Franco-Prussian war memorial displaying a bust of Kaiser Wilhelm I stands opposite the fountain, there is a pleasant stroll down Bachstrasse alongside a little stream. Then take the tree-lined road that leads north to Baden-Baden from here, pausing in the busy, colourful village of Renchen to see the statues of the poet and writer Johann Jakob Christoph von Grimmelshausen. In the first, by the fountain, he is depicted raising his hat to passers-by in a friendly fashion. The second statue just beyond the church is

more conventional. The peacefulness of Renchen today contrasts with Grimmelshausen's own savage era. He was born in 1621 and died at Renchen in 1676, experiencing in his lifetime all the horrors of the Thirty Years' War, for Croatian soldiers kidnapped him just as it was heating up and he was forced to serve and suffer as a boy soldier. He ended the war as clerk to his regiment. All the savagery he had seen inspired him to write the work for which he is known, *Simplicius Simplicissimus*, a biting satire on the cruelty of his time.

A few kilometres further on the road passes through the larger town of Achern, filled with hotels and restaurants and graced with a pedestrianized shopping centre, a market square with a fountain, and a church in a square shaded with chestnut trees. The people here seem to be proud of what to my mind is the curiously ungainly chapel of St Nikolaus, built in the fourteenth century and topped with a sixteenth-century tower. There is also a rather pompous memorial to Grand Duke Leopold, ruler of Baden between 1830 and 1852, with a lady holding a circlet of palm leaves over his head and a wreath round his waist. This Grand Duke was evidently much revered, for when Mary Shelley and her friends arrived at Darmstadt in 1842 the town was eagerly expecting a visit from Leopold. Mary recorded that in their hotel 'the whole of the private rooms were prepared for him, and we were shut out from all, except the common eating-room – of course, redolent with smoke'. What was worse, the party found it difficult to get any service, since the waiters were continually rushing to the window to see if their Grand Duke had arrived.

Leopold seems to have presided over a grand duchy

Winter in the Black Forest near the quiet village of Renchen, home of the seventeenth-century novelist and poet Johann Jakob Christoph von Grimmelshausen.

with a lively political life. A short time later the Baden parliament was deeply divided over whether capital punishment should be abolished. The progressives and the conservatives came to a compromise: the death penalty was retained, but in future would be administered not by hanging but by the more humane guillotine.

About 350 metres before you reach Sasbach on the road out of Achern to the north, watch out for the monument to Louis XIV's famous marshal Henri de la Tour d'Auvergne, Vicomte de Turenne, who reconquered Alsace for the French and was killed here by a bullet on 27 July 1675. An avenue of pine trees on the right leads to the spot where he fell and to a granite obelisk inscribed *La France à Turenne*. Sasbach also boasts a splendid eighteenth-century church, not quite so great as that at Appenweier but well worth stopping for, and curiously dedicated to St Brigid of Kildare. This Irish princess and saint, one of whose attributes was the useful ability to turn her bath-water into beer, recalls the Scottish and Irish monks who founded a monastery here in 750. Inside the church the Lamb of God sits on a seven-sealed book on top of the tabernacle.

Drive on through Ottersweier, whose town hall was once a Jesuit college and whose gothic parish church (except for parts of the west towers) was well restored in the nineteenth century. The church square has a modern statue of St John the Baptist, water cascading from his hand, his hair streaming in the wind, looking for all the world as if he has just taken a dip in the little stream that runs nearby. In summer boxes of flowers are everywhere. And just outside the village is a baroque church, once renowned for a statue of Our Lady known as Maria Linden. True to its name the church of Maria Linden is surrounded by lime trees and more unexpectedly accompanied by a welcome restaurant.

Setting out once more along a road lined with fruit trees and vines, the route north passes through villages

Left The French field marshal Turenne was killed in action in 1675 near this fruitful spot outside Sasbach.

Above A lake in the Black Forest near Bühl, a town noted for the excellence of its fruit.

and towns washed with streams running down from the Black Forest. On a hot summer's day it is worth turning into Steinbach – the birthplace of Erwin and his son Jean who created the west front of Strasbourg cathedral – to take advantage of the open-air swimming-pool. There is also a refreshing wine cellar here and a café selling the rich cream cakes that have bloated many of the clients thronging Baden-Baden a few kilometres away.

Turn right to the spa along the B500, past the splendid railway station which gives a hint of the gorgeous architecture to come. Fine parks, great fountains and sophisticated shops all testify to the fact that you can become rich if you tell self-indulgent people that you can make them fit and well again. Mark Twain resented paying out good cash here. Baden-Baden, he decided, was an inane town filled with sham, petty fraud and snobbery. 'The shop-keeper there swindles you if he can, and insults you whether he succeeds in swindling you or not,' he decided. Still, the baths cured him of rheumatism. Mark Twain regretted that he had left only rheumatism behind, and not something catching.

His fellow American Henry Adams gave a more favourable report, describing Baden-Baden as morally 'delicious', since the women he saw there made his hair stand on end. Then as now, the town was much more than a spot to relieve one's aches and pains. In 1862 Édouard Bénazet built a baroque theatre in the Kurpark, used for music as well as drama and now the venue for concerts which are almost as celebrated as the casino. Brahms, who lived in Baden between 1865 and 1874, was one of the many famous musicians attracted here; his house at no. 85 Maximilianstrasse is now a museum of his life and art.

None the less, Baden-Baden is still known primarily for its curative waters, renowned since Roman times. You can still visit the baths in Römerplatz which the Emperor Caracalla constructed here in the early third century and which had no successors until the first Kurhaus was built in 1765. Enlarged in 1824 by Friedrich Weinbrenner when the spa began to prosper, it now incorporates restaurants and the celebrated casino which Jacques and Édouard Bénazet designed in 1854 as well as the baths themselves. Édouard was fascinated by English gardens and the long Lichten-taler Allee leading from his baroque theatre to the fourteenth- and fifteenth-century buildings of the Cistercian abbey of Lichtental is supposed to be based on the English style.

Baden-Baden is scarcely 12 kilometres from the Rhine. To drive back into France take the D4, cross the river and turn right at the T-junction along the N63 to the little town of Seltz, where the River Sauer meets the Seltzbach. The fortified camp established by the Romans here was chosen as the site of a Benedictine monastery set up in 991 with the blessing (and money) of the Empress Adelaide in memory of her husband Otto, founder of the Holy Roman Empire. She herself was buried at Seltz, but the Rhine overflowed and carried her body away. Her modern statue stands in front of the church, itself now partly modern (since the little town was much damaged in World War II), though the flamboyant gothic choir and transept as well as a baroque high altar have been preserved from the older building. Seltz also managed to survive the war with its mid nineteenth-century town hall and several picturesque half-timbered houses still intact.

Eleven kilometres north of Seltz is the frontier town of Lauterbourg, situated at the north-eastern tip of France where the River Lauter flows into the Rhine. Few places have had a more tumultuous history. From Roman times when it was first fortified Lauterbourg has been continually contested and attacked. After almost total destruction in the Thirty Years' War Vauban rebuilt its ramparts on behalf of Louis XIV,

Forest-clad hills sheltering the celebrated spa of Baden-Baden.

Left **An elegant colonnade in Baden-Baden, where the rich come to repair the ravages of an over-indulgent lifestyle.**

Above **Classical serenity in the Schlossgarten at Karlsruhe, north of Baden-Baden, a city created in the nineteenth century by the architect Friedrich Weinbrenner.**

only for the town to pass to Prussia in 1793. Also caught up in the Franco-Prussian war at the end of the next century, Lauterbourg again suffered terribly in World War II. Lauterbourg's architecture proclaims this long military past. An ancient tower and some of its medieval walls remain and some of Vauban's defences still stand, including a gate with the emblem of the Sun King. And in spite of its history of warfare you can still see lovely renaissance houses and an eighteenth-century church here.

Drive west from Lauterbourg along the D3 with the earth ramparts, retaining walls, forts and redoubts of the so-called Wissembourg lines, created by the military architect Villars in the mid eighteenth century, visible as a 20-kilometre line away to the north. Wissembourg itself lies 17 kilometres from Lauterbourg, a delicious town surrounded by the remnants of its medieval fortifications as well as three stern towers from a fourteenth-century château. In 1720 it offered refuge to the exiled king of Poland, Stanislas Leczinka, and you can still see the eighteenth-century mansion he lived in, now known as the Hôpital Stanislas. This is where Louis XV came in 1725 to seek the hand of his daughter Maria. The town is packed with many other superb buildings dating from the late Middle Ages to the eighteenth century, including a fifteenth-century salt-house with an immense roof and no fewer than four granaries. There are also three partly romanesque churches, of which SS Peter and Paul is one of the greatest in Alsace and certainly second only to Strasbourg cathedral in size. The huge wall-painting of St Christopher that was uncovered here in 1967 turned out to be the largest fresco in France. Those with more baroque tastes will prefer the eighteenth-century church of Mary of the Seven Sorrows, where Maria Leczinka liked to worship.

A reproving look from a Karlsruhe lady.

A moment of savagery amidst classical harmony: Samson slays a lion in the Schlossgarten, Karlsruhe.

Wissembourg is also an excellent centre from which to explore the nature park of the northern Vosges, with riding and guided walks on offer and the opportunity to hunt and fish in season. Then drive south from Wissembourg to Haguenau through the Haguenau forest, the largest in Alsace. Once thought to be sacred, its beeches, pines, hornbeams and oaks are now criss-crossed with well-signposted walks. Haguenau itself lies on the River Moder, which snakes its way through the town. The road from the north brings you almost immediately to the church of St Nicolas, with its thirteenth-century choir and fifteenth-century ogival vaulting. The exquisite mid eighteenth-century stalls were transferred here from the Cistercian abbey of Neubourg.

I cannot discover why Haguenau has such a wealth

of churches. One of the finest is St George, where the nave dates from the twelfth century and the octagonal romanesque tower contains the two oldest bells in Alsace, cast in 1268. Two gems in this church are the reredos over the high altar painted in 1497, which depicts the Last Judgment, and the gothic pulpit sculpted by Veit Wagner in the sixteenth century. Another church, the fifteenth-century St Sepulchre, can lay claim to one of the oddest curiosities of Alsace: a carving of Jesus being tortured in a wine-press. The Jewish cemetery and a classical synagogue designed in 1840 are religious memorials of another kind, reminders that Alsace once sheltered a sizeable Jewish population. Look out too for fine ironwork and beautifully tiled roofs, especially in the pedestrianized heart of the town.

From Haguenau the forested N63 runs east for 14 kilometres to Soufflenheim, an apparently drab little town until you spot that it is the heart of the traditional Alsatian pottery industry. Potters set themselves up here at least as early as the twelfth century, and today you can watch their successors in the workshops crowded round the church, where they create superb flower-pots, salad bowls, vases, jugs, carafes, baking dishes and moulds for cakes and mousses, traditionally decorated with flowers and leaves. Needless to say the potters are only too happy to sell their wares to passing visitors. The parish church which stands in their midst

is remarkable for the fact that, contrary to tradition, its altar is at the north rather than the east end.

To reach the little town of Sessenheim to the south-east leave by the Grand'Rue west of the church, turning right into rue de la Gare, and seek the D138 and D737. Although pretty but otherwise unremarkable, Sessenheim is of interest for the Goethe museum in the former Napoleonic guard-house, set up here because the young student fell disastrously in love with Frédérique Brion in the town. The affair was more damaging for the girl, the daughter of Pastor Brion of Sessenheim, than for Goethe. They had been introduced by his friend Weyland when Goethe was a Strasbourg undergraduate of 22 and she was 19. Goethe, who loved fancy dress, first appeared at Sessenheim in the garb of a poverty-stricken student of theology. Instantly attracted to the young Frédérique, he speedily returned to Strasbourg and borrowed his landlord's son's best clothes in order to make a better impression. He and Frédérique took a moonlight stroll

Left **Can anyone tell the time from the complex astronomical clock at Haguenau? Does anyone wish to, during the town's annual gastronomic and beer festivals?**

Right **Traditional Alsatian pottery from Soufflenheim. Terracotta was developed here during the Bronze Age, though today's techniques for firing, glazing and painting the local clay derive from the twelfth century.**

together and the girl was overwhelmed. So at first was Goethe. Only one of his letters to her survives and it is suffused with passion. 'Could it be that you, so tender and so good, have not the slightest inclination towards me, the one who holds you so dear?' he asks, adding, 'You would not at all believe how much the city's noise grates on my ears after your delicious country joys.' Frédérique's mother soon brought her on a visit to Strasbourg, and the love was further enflamed.

Goethe would ride headlong to Sessenheim to see his *amoureuse*, recounting in verse:

Quick throbbed my heart – mount horse; away!
Sharp as a warrior to the fray . . .
The night brought countless monsters dire
But still I not one fear did meet.
My brain was like a raging fire,
My heart did melt in fervent heat.

One of Goethe's early masterpieces, *Willkommen und Abschied*, expresses his misery at parting from Frédérique. At Easter they sat together in the pastor's pew in Sessenheim church, and Goethe was overjoyed that Frédérique's father's sermon was an excessively long one.

Soon he realized that he was living a myth. Goethe was not truly in love with the real Frédérique. Alas, the real Frédérique was in love with Goethe. How to break off such a relationship? In his *Dichtung und Wahrheit* Goethe tells how in his 'confused cravings' he still could not resist seeing Frédérique one more time. 'These were painful days,' he confessed, 'though I scarcely remember them now. When I reached down from my horse to take her hand, there were tears in her eyes. I felt deeply miserable.' Only when he left Strasbourg for Frankfurt did he dare write to her to explain that there was no future together for them. Her

The parsonage at Sessenheim is where Goethe loved and then betrayed the pastor's daughter.

answer almost broke his own cruel heart. 'The same hand, the same mind, the same feeling which had been nurtured for me and by me was writing this letter,' he perceived. 'For the first time I now realised what loss she had suffered, but I could see no way of making it good, or even of alleviating it.'

Johann Wolfgang Goethe was to break the hearts of other women, as he had already done before he met Frédérique. Ten years after leaving Strasbourg he decided to see his forsaken sweetheart once again and rode once more into Sessenheim. Pastor Brion and his family received the self-centred genius with far more courtesy than he deserved. He stayed overnight, even walking Frédérique once more by moonlight. They recalled happier times, visiting every one of their old arbors. 'I felt quite relieved,' said Goethe. Frédérique, he wrote, 'loved me in the past more dearly than I

A half-timbered house in the charming hamlet of Sessenheim.

merited and more than other women on whom I have devoted much passion and faithfulness.' He added, 'I was forced to leave her in a moment when it almost cost the girl her life. She passed lightly over the fact.' The next day Goethe rode back to Strasbourg to call on another ex-sweetheart, Lili Schönemann. Frédérique Brion never fell in love again and never married.

Memorials to Goethe and Frédérique Brion and the tombstones of Pastor Brion and other members of his family which line the church wall are not the only sad mementoes at Sessenheim. As the graves round the church tell so eloquently, the war of the Spanish Succession ravaged the little spot, and 143 of its inhabitants succumbed in the previous century when the plague hit Europe in 1633.

From Sessenheim take the D300 south-west over the Rhine plain towards Strasbourg, turning right after about a dozen kilometres along the minor road leading to Brumath. As you go through the village of Weyersheim about half-way there notice the colour of the walls of the houses. Following a dying tradition in Alsace they are painted blue, not white, for this is a Catholic village and blue is the colour of Our Lady.

Although now sleepily rural, Brumath itself was a place of considerable importance in Roman times, one of the key stations for controlling lower Alsace. Then in the thirteenth century it became the capital of the Landgravate of the region. Slipping into relative obscurity since the Middle Ages, it nevertheless produced the Alsatian poet and painter Gustave Stoskopf, who died in 1944 at the age of 75.

In most of the places we have passed through it is possible to eat well. At Haguenau, for instance, they are proud of their fruit tarts, hold a gastronomic festival in the last week of August and another one devoted to hops on the first Sunday in September. At Brumath the onions are famed for their delicacy and celebrated on 24 September every year. What is important is that you do not leave this curious area of two countries without enjoying a German as well as a French meal. Among the numerous restaurants in Strasbourg seek out one whose menu offers *Lewer-knepfles*, the liver dumplings found in both Alsace and Germany but cooked in Alsace infinitely better than across the Rhine.

Brumath's eighteenth-century château now houses a Gallo-Roman museum, an illustration of the fact that this hospitable spot has been inhabited for over two millennia.

Cologne

Brühl

Vorgebirge

Siebengebirge

Schwarz-Rheindorf

Bonn

Bad Godesberg

Rolandseck

Oberwinter

Remagen

Ahr

Sinzig

Bad Breisig

Brohl-Lützing

Lake Laacher

Weissenthurm

Andernach

Rhine

Eifel

Koblenz

Bopparder Hamm

Kapellen-Stolzenfels

Rhens

Spay

Boppard

Bad Salzig

Hirzenach

Moselle

St Goar

Lorelei

Oberwesel

Kaub

Taunus

Bacharach

Niederheimbach

Trechtingshausen

Rheingau

Gaulsheim

Wiesbaden

Main

Bingen

Ingelheim

Finthen

Gau-Algesheim

Mainz

Nahe

Weizbach

Selz

0   5   10 km

N

Cologne

Bonn

Koblenz

Mainz

Frankfurt

Mannheim

France

Karlsruhe

Baden-Baden

Strasbourg

W. Germany

Colmar

Rhine

Mulhouse

Lake Constance

Basle

Switzerland

4
The Romance
of the Middle Rhine

Mainz – Bingen – Bacharach – Oberwesel –
St Goar – Boppard – Rhens – Koblenz –
Andernach – Bad Breisig – Sinzig – Bad Godesberg –
Bonn – Brühl – Cologne

Although this fertile, much fought-over stretch of country includes Mainz and its satellite towns as well as the city of Koblenz, this is an entrancing stretch of the Rhine with little villages nestling in sunny hollows and majestic views to distant peaks. Continually the scene changes. Around Mainz itself the countryside is gentle, a landscape of orchards and vineyards. Northwards from Bingen the terrain becomes wilder, as the Rhine valley narrows to resemble a gorge. The railways which have been running parallel to the river now have to tunnel their way through the cliffs on either side. Steep crags rise from the water, crowned with a string of romantic castles and with once-mighty fortresses which fire the historical imagination with their ruined melancholy. 'What lives did the ancient inhabitants of these crumbling ruins lead!' exclaimed Mary Shelley as she sailed down the river over a century ago. 'The occupation of the men was war; that of the women to hope, to fear, to pray, and to embroider.'

Armies have surged back and forth over this part of the Rhine. The fortresses were built by barons and knights who hoped to exploit the river traffic as well as to give themselves a secure base. The wars of the Middle Ages followed by the Thirty Years' War and the depredations of the French wrought havoc here and have left us these monuments to men's ambitions and occasional savagery. The tumbling walls set beneath towering crags have also given rise to many legends and inspired ecstatic poetry, such as these lines by Walter Savage Landor:

> Swiftly we sail along thy stream,
> War-stricken Rhine! and evening's gleam
> Shows us, throughout its course,
> The gaping scars (on either side,
> On every cliff) of guilty pride
> And unavailing force.

This poet's imagination conjured up castles where the dungeons were too deep and the towers too high for love ever to hear the sighs of the rejected or for law to avenge the groans of the abused.

If the savagery of the Middle Ages seems to peer down from these mossy turrets and from castellated walls now covered in ivy, medieval piety looks out from the ancient chapels and former convents high up in the forests. Here too is the gentler charm of vineyards and wine villages, of half-timbered houses and the crumbling fortifications of little towns. The middle Rhine itself is a bustling traffic artery, where ferries ply back and forth with tourists and sightseers, and where inns serve hearty German meals accompanied with elegant wines and satisfying beers. Many others – Herman Melville, Victor Hugo and Goethe among them – have followed the route I take here, their experiences sometimes echoing and sometimes contrasting with my own, but always vivid in their evocation of the landscape and its history.

Mainz stands on the left bank of the Rhine, opposite its confluence with the River Main. It is worth taking the time to cross the water here as the loveliest view of the city is from the far bank, with the enormous six-towered cathedral overshadowing the charming succession of buildings which line the river. This mountainous building on Leichhof Platz with its romanesque east end was founded on the site of an earlier church in 975 by one of the most powerful archbishops in German history, Willigis, who doubled up his archiepiscopal duties with the all-powerful office of chancellor of the Holy Roman Empire, the collection of independent princely states which made up the German nation. For centuries his successors played the same role, becoming also prince-electors and primates of Germany, but none was more powerful than Willigis.

Mainz was already well established when the cathedral was begun. The strategic advantages of the site were recognized early and there was a Celtic camp here dedicated to the god Mogon. When the Romans took over in 38 BC they thought this Celtic deity was Apollo. To the south-west of the city, in the suburb of Zahlbach, you can still see the remains of the Roman aqueduct which brought water to the camp from a spring 5 kilometres away. Another legacy of this period is the lovely 9-metre column dedicated to the god Jupiter, set up here as a thanksgiving for the Emperor Nero's recovery from an illness. It stands between the eighteenth-century headquarters of the Teutonic knights and the delicious rococo church of St Peter (or rather a copy stands here; the original is now in the regional museum of the middle Rhine, which is also in Mainz).

Mogontiacum, as the Romans called Mainz, became the headquarters of the 22nd Roman legion in the second century AD. Then the Romans withdrew and their fragile monuments were destroyed by the barbarians. A new Christianization of Germany inspired by an Englishman, St Boniface, raised Mainz from its ruins.

Boniface's zeal and energy were astonishing. So was his courage. Born around 680 at Crediton in England's Devonshire and educated by monks, he first decided to missionize Friesland (now the northern part of the Netherlands). Undeterred by his lack of success here, he went to Rome, where Pope Gregory II made him a bishop and charged him with converting the pagans of Germany. This time Boniface was luckier and succeeded in pulling off a remarkable coup. At Geismar he discovered that the pagans worshipped a huge oak tree dedicated to their god Thor. In the presence of a vast crowd, Boniface announced his intention of hewing it down, risking of course death at the hands of an angry Thor. He had scarcely begun to strike at the tree with his axe when it split into four and fell to the ground. Boniface consummated his triumph by using its wood to build a chapel dedicated to St Peter.

The pope now charged the saint with establishing sees throughout Germany. He brought English monks to the Continent and founded monasteries for them, one of which – at Fulda – became the greatest in northern Europe. The delighted pope next made him apostolic delegate for Gaul as well as Germany, and Boniface's importance was recognized when he crowned Pepin king of the Franks. In 747 this

The early twentieth-century Christuskirche at Mainz, now used as a concert hall, rises beyond a copy of a third-century Roman arch.

remarkable man made Mainz his metropolitan see. From this moment the city's fortunes began to revive, though Boniface soon tired of staying in one place and in 754 set out on a second attempt to reconvert the Frieslanders. Alas, they murdered him.

His successors as archbishops of Mainz brought wealth and prestige to the city. By the thirteenth century Mainz was so prosperous that it was known as 'Golden Mainz', or *Aurea Moguntia*. In 1254 a rich Mainz merchant, Arnold Walpod, set up a league of cities along the Rhine to defend the river trade from brigands, and soon some eighty towns had joined. It was in this golden age that much of the present glory of Mainz cathedral was created, though the building was continually enriched for centuries afterwards.

In consequence this great church, its six towers rising above the half-timbered houses of the old city, is a blend of all kinds and conditions of architecture. The romanesque basilica has additions in both thirteenth- and nineteenth-century gothic, as well as baroque and renaissance features. Its largest dome, for example, is built partly in the renaissance style, partly in the baroque. We owe the east tower – a fine example of nineteenth-century gothic – indirectly to Napoleon. It was rebuilt in 1870 after the artillery of the French army had demolished it in 1793. The west tower, whose present form emerged over five centuries, is even more ornate, a blend of gothic and baroque. Walk to the square on the north-west side simply to admire the sheer bulk of the whole building as it rises above the town.

This architectural *mélange* in no way prepares you for the fantastic interior of the cathedral. Go in by the thirteenth-century Marktportal, whose bronze doors are a thousand years old. Fifty-six pillars support the basilica, many of them sculpted or painted with saints. Here are baroque and rococo stalls, renaissance altars and medieval funerary monuments. For an example of late medieval artistic piety seek out the magical gilded winged altarpiece carved around 1515 in a chapel half-

way down the north side. A crowned Virgin Mary, carrying her chubby-cheeked child, stands between two mitred bishops. Behind her two angels hold a rich embroidered cloth.

Because of her long blue robe you cannot see whether this Virgin Mary is wearing shoes or not. Was this, I wonder, the statue before which (according to an old Mainz legend) a ragged impoverished fiddler decided to play, after spending a cold winter's day making music in the streets of the city without collecting a single coin? Since the sound of his violin had failed to touch the hearts or pockets of the passers-by, he crept into the cathedral and poured out his woes to the Blessed Virgin. Then he began to play for her. Suddenly Mary lifted her foot, took off her golden slipper and handed it to the poor old man. Overjoyed he longed to keep the gift, but as he was starving he took it to the market the next morning. Of course he was instantly accused of stealing the treasure of the cathedral. The fiddler was sentenced to death. On the day of his execution he asked one boon: to be allowed to play for the Virgin Mary again. The city fathers granted his dying prayer and once again the fiddler's music filled the cathedral. When he had finished playing, the statue raised her other foot, took off her second golden slipper and gave it to the old man. His guards were dumbfounded, he was pardoned, and the cathedral clergy provided for him for the rest of his life. Just in case the miraculous statue should take it into her head to be bountiful again, the Virgin Mary's golden slippers were locked away in the cathedral treasure chest.

The twentieth century has added its quota of fine art to this great church. The high altar dates from 1960, its modern cross created 15 years later by an artist named Zeugner. In the thousand-year-old crypt the relics of 22 saints lie in a delicate modern reliquary, fashioned in gold in the same year as the altar.

To add to this wealth of statues and sculptures, Mainz cathedral also houses the tombs of no fewer than

44 of the 84 archbishops and bishops of Mainz. Some of these tombs are splendid, a reflection of the stature of the men they commemorate, two of them – the last resting-places of the archbishops Johann Philip and Lothar Franz von Schönborn – designed by that greatest of all baroque architects, Balthasar Neumann. My own favourite among these princes of the church, Wilhelm Emmanuel von Ketteler, lived in the nineteenth century and lies here in a marble tomb.

A Prussian civil servant, Ketteler was so appalled at the way the Prussian state was coercing the Catholic Church (even to the extent of imprisoning the archbishop of Cologne in 1837 because he refused to accept the state's line on mixed marriages), that he resigned and was ordained priest. His pastoral work among the poor opened his eyes to their low physical as well as spiritual state. An aristocrat himself, he began to attack his peers for being far more concerned about their titles than their duties, proclaiming his views in the cathedral in 1848 when he described neglect of the poor as 'a perpetual crime against nature'. Two years later he returned as bishop of Mainz, his zeal to reform society not one whit lessened. A stream of books, pamphlets and sermons set out his demands: child labour must be banned; women and young girls should be relieved of hours of drudgery in factories; the workers needed holidays and shorter working hours; their demands for more pay were justified; the evils of economic liberalism should be exposed as setting men and women against each other. This doughty champion of the poor died in 1877.

Another celebrated citizen lies entombed in the cathedral cloisters, commemorated by an eighteenth-century copy of the stone under which his body was laid in 1318. His name was Heinrich von Meissen (after the town in central Germany where he was born around 1260), but everyone called him *Frauenlob*, 'extoller of ladies', a nickname which he gained after successfully defending the word *Vrowe*, 'lady' in middle high German, in a poetry contest. His rival Regenbogen preferred the less flattering *Wip*, or woman.

Frauenlob settled in Mainz in 1312 and here he founded the first school of *Meistersingers*, poets who followed his example in writing verse filled with ingenious metaphors, theological musings and double meanings. His own greatest work, the *Marienleich*, was written in praise of the Blessed Virgin Mary. The citizens of Mainz are proud of Frauenlob, and in 1852 commissioned the sculptor Schwanthaler to create the monument now in the cathedral cloisters which honours him.

On a corner of the cathedral square stands the city's Gutenberg museum, grandiosely dubbed the 'museum of world printing'. Johann Gutenberg was born in Mainz around 1400, the illegitimate son of a clergyman named Gensfleisch and a lady named Gutenberg. He is credited with inventing printing, but the truth is slightly more complicated. Printing with engraved wooden blocks was in fact common long before he was born, and Gutenberg's first achievement in the field was to perceive that a wine-press could be adapted to ease the work. His greatest invention was to work out how to cast separate letters, so the printer could set up a page in movable type rather than laboriously producing it as a whole on a wooden block as before.

His museum, partly housed in a lovely seventeenth-century renaissance inn, Zum Römischen Kaiser, contains a replica of Gutenberg's hand-press in a reconstruction of an early printing workshop. Its most prized exhibit is a copy of the Gutenberg Bible, printed on parchment around 1445. There are only 47 left in the world, and this one retains its original binding.

Close by in Gutenbergplatz is the house of German wines, *Das Haus des Deutschen Weines*, where you can also eat, its façade decorated with the coats of arms of the wine districts of Germany. Customers here ought to choose the superb wines produced from the slopes of the Taunus mountains across the river, an area scarcely 24 kilometres long known as the Rheingau. Goethe,

who spent happy autumnal days wandering in this region, would have agreed. He ended his account of these travels by quoting two lines from a song composed by Matthäus Claudius, a journalist friend:

> *Am Rhein! Am Rhein!*
> *Da wachsen uns're Reben!*
> (By the Rhine! By the Rhine!
> 'Tis here we grow our wine.)

Goethe was a connoisseur of the region's wine, observing sagely that its quality depends not simply on the situation of the vineyard but also on a late vintage. As he noted, this meant that the poor and the wealthy are always at odds with each other, the poor preferring an abundant, early harvest, the wealthy a good, late one.

If you are not planning to eat in the *Haus* but would simply relish a drink, try a delicate Rheingau Riesling, looking out for the word *Erzeugerabfüllung* on the label, which indicates that the wine is estate bottled. Whereas the Rieslings produced in Alsace have all the sugar fermented out, so as to make a strong, dry white wine with a high alcohol content, Rieslings from the Rheingau (and from the upper Moselle too) are sweeter and much lighter in body. Their alcohol content can be as little as 8 per cent. The descriptions on the label – Kabinett, Spätlese and Auslese – indicate an increasing and aromatic sweetness in the wine. All these Rheingau Rieslings come in a brown bottle, as opposed to the green bottles of the Moselle.

If you do plan to eat, set aside the Rieslings in favour of the wine known as Schloss Johannisberger, which is stronger and more capable of matching the Mainz cuisine. The sturdy German dishes on offer here include *Handkas mit Musik*, a snack made of cheese and finely chopped onions drenched in vinegar and

---

Caryatids strain under the weight of a Mainz portico.

oil. All the many *Weinstuben* in the old city's narrow half-timbered streets offer this pungent delicacy.

When Goethe visited Mainz he brooded on the savage military past of this part of the Rhine and urged the citizens to establish a military school, conscious of the devastating French invasion in 1793 which he had watched. 'Even in the midst of peace everyone with his eyes open is reminded of war', he wrote. 'Activity alone will drive away fear and anxiety; and what displays of the science of fortification and siege have not been witnessed over and over again here! Every trench, every hill would speak instructively to the young soldier, and daily and hourly impress upon him that this is, perhaps, the most important point where German patriotism will have to steel itself to firmest resolves.' Eventually Goethe's words were heeded, and Mainz became an important military centre – to its cost in World War II.

Grievously damaged in 1945, much of the city has been most sensitively reconstructed. Charming fountains stand in front of baroque houses. In Schillerstrasse the Bilhildis fountain almost washes the walls of the baroque Erthaler Hof, named after Baron Philipp Christian von Erthal who paid for it. Not far away on the south side of Schillerplatz rises the elegant rococo Osteiner Hof, built some 15 years later in 1749. Many features of the city have their own rich history. The renaissance fountain in the market square, for instance, one of the prettiest in Germany, was placed there in 1526 by Archbishop Albrecht von Brandenburg to celebrate the defeat of the Peasants' Rising in the previous year.

Mainz was walled around the year 1200, and two fine remains of these fortifications still stand beside the Rhine: the extremely pretty Eiserne gate, and the slenderer gateway-tower known as the Holzturm. Two buildings close by along the river bank – the new town hall and the Rheingoldhalle – are a direct contrast. Designed by the Danish architect Arne Jacobsen in the 1960s and 1970s, the town hall is made of reinforced

concrete and clad in Norwegian marble, looking to me quite out of place in a city on the left bank of the Rhine.

When Victor Hugo visited Mainz he was preoccupied not with military matters but with the beauty of the women who plied the river boats. (Byron too had warmed to these 'peasant girls, with deep blue eyes'.) Victor Hugo also observed that the citizens possessed enormous vigour, a quality he attributed to the influence of the Rhine itself. 'People walk, they talk, they push, they pull, they sell, they buy, they shout, they sing, above all they *live*, in every quarter, in every house, in every street.' They still do.

Going north from Mainz Bundesstrasse 9 along the left bank of the Rhine runs through a succession of exquisite villages set in fertile fruit and wine country. Follow Binger Strasse from the city's central station past the vast buildings of the university, watching for the signs to Ingelheim. The route shortly passes through Finthen, where the Romans discovered a spring to supply their aqueduct with water. Then the road begins to rise, with splendid views across the river to the whole Rheingau stretching away on the other bank. From this vantage point it is easy to work out precisely why the wine of this region is so fine, for the great river has momentarily turned west-southwest. Vineyards on the far bank stretch up the south-facing slopes of the Taunus mountains, nurtured in deep brown earth and bathed by the sun. Experts claim that some warmth is even reflected from the Rhine itself. And the river helps in other ways too. As the very end of the wine harvest approaches, it throws up a mist which rises up through the vineyards and begins to rot the remaining grapes. This last fruit of the year is carefully picked to produce the sweetest dessert wines, Beerenauslese and Trockenbeerenauslese.

The road then descends again, passing the obelisk at the hamlet of Steig which declares that Napoleon Bonaparte was responsible for building it. Only a military megalomaniac could have enforced such a straight line, running 28 kilometres as far as Bingen. Shortly afterwards you reach Ingelheim on the River Selz. Like most others in this region, this is an important wine town, but it is unusual for producing red wine (the Ingelheim Spätburgunder) as well as white. If you come here at the end of September or the beginning of October, you will be able to enjoy the annual red wine festival.

Ingelheim was once well defended, and in the southern part of the town the Burg church (Burgkirche) still nestles in the shelter of massive fortifications. Here too are the fragments of the palace which Charlemagne built in the second half of the eighth century, now circling the thirteenth-century church. As for the fountain in front of the town hall, Georges Arnold who designed it in 1811 was also the engineer who built the Napoleonic road we are following. Take a 30-minute detour from Ingelheim to see the romantic ruins of Schloss Waldeck, high up above the valley with superb views over the river. Close by stands the Bismarck tower, rising some 205 metres over Upper Ingelheim.

These towns and villages in the fertile land along the river are often separated by scarcely 5 kilometres. Next comes Gau-Algesheim (reached by a slight detour along the B41), known for its asparagus as well as the inevitable wine and fruit. For visitors its delights include a flamboyant gothic town hall, a tower of 1340 and a splendid tomb in the church commemorating Konrad von Waldeck who died in 1463. Three kilometres further on you reach Gaulsheim and once again there are glimpses of the river. High on a rocky promontory across the Rhine is the megalomanic statue of Germania, set up here to commemorate the re-establishment of the German empire under Bismarck

---

A painted house in the market square at Mainz, which is also graced by a fountain given to the city by Archbishop Albrecht von Brandenburg in 1526.

Left An island in the Rhine near Ingelheim, a town where you can sample one of this region's rare red wines, the Spätburgunder.

Above Burg Klopp, Bingen. The fearsome twelfth-century castle was restored in the early nineteenth century and is now a museum of local history.

129

A Bingen wine merchant celebrates his city by painting St Martin's church on the left side of his house and Burg Klopp on the right.

and Kaiser Wilhelm I in 1871. Less arrogant is the convent of St Hildegard on the Rochusberg, 110 metres above the river. Park your car here and walk up through the cool woods for an hour and a half or so to a gothic chapel built in 1895. The superb views are worth the climb.

St Hildegard was one of the most remarkable of a series of Christian mystics produced by medieval Germany. Even as a child she experienced extraordinary visions. 'Once I saw a light so bright that I was terrified', she wrote, 'but my childish shyness stopped me telling anyone about it.' Later she wrote down virtually everything she learned, mingling useful information on medicine with improving lives of the saints and accounts of her visions. She saw

devils who disguised themselves as sparkling lights but were later transformed into black coals. She insisted that these visions came to her when she was fully awake, not when she was in a trance. Her fame grew, and eventually she was appointed a Benedictine abbess and founded her convent here by the Rhine in 1147. She died in 1179 in some ill-favour with the papacy, for she had allowed an excommunicated man to be buried in the convent cemetery. Though the convent was for a time placed under a papal interdict, St Hildegard doggedly refused to change her mind, for she argued the man had received the last sacraments of the church just before his death and therefore deserved Christian burial.

Drive on from Gaulsheim past the Rochusberg to reach Bingen, built on a triangle of land between the Rhine and its tributary the Nahe. Vineyards rise gently beyond the town. Bingen is dominated by the massive feudal Burg Klopp, a great castle perched 128 metres above the Rhine. Although seemingly medieval, the original building was largely destroyed in 1711 and the *Schloss* we see today is a reconstruction of 1879, pleasingly surrounded by rock gardens. Far older is the church of St Martin in the town, a fifteenth-century building based on an eleventh-century crypt. More ancient still is the little chapel on the bridge over the River Nahe, one of the oldest such buildings in Germany and constructed probably as early as the tenth century.

In the Rhine itself stands the romantic eleventh-century Mouse Tower, rising from a rocky perch in the middle of the river. The name Mouse Tower almost certainly derives from *Mautturm*, which means toll tower; but the linguistic confusion has led to a pleasing tale. Tradition holds that the poor of Mainz were cruelly oppressed by a certain Bishop Hatto in the tenth century. Although his granaries were full, the

Dancing girls on a charming capital in Bingen.

starving crowded around them in vain. One day, however, it appeared that the bishop had relented; everyone in need was invited to come to one of his great barns. But when the poor arrived, their stomachs rumbling in anticipation, he locked them inside and set fire to the barn. Robert Southey's poem continues the story:

'I'faith, 'tis an excellent bonfire!' quoth he,
'And the country is greatly obliged to me,
For ridding it in these times forlorn,
Of rats that only consume the corn.'

So then to his palace returnèd he,
And he sat down to supper merrily;
And he slept that night like an innocent man,
But Bishop Hatto never slept again.

When Hatto rose the following morning and entered the great hall of the episcopal palace he noticed with a tremor that rats had eaten his portrait out of its frame. Then one of his tenant farmers arrived with the startling information that other rats had eaten all his corn. Soon another servant came running with the news that ten thousand rats were on their way to wreak vengeance on the bishop.

'I'll go to my tower on the Rhine,' replied he,
' 'Tis the safest place in Germany;
The walls are high and the shores are steep,
And the stream is strong and the water deep.'

The rats pursued him there. By their thousands they swam the river, as the bishop fearfully told his beads. Gnawing their way in, the beasts set upon the evil Hatto. Southey's poem ends:

They have whetted their teeth against the stones,
And now they pick the Bishop's bones;
They gnawed the flesh from every limb,
For they were sent to do judgement on him.

No such horrors assailed Dorothy and William Wordsworth as they travelled through the soft and open scenery that borders the river here in 1820. She wrote that they 'were reminded of Windermere, and of the fields of England; – images of pleasure – but it was not without regret that we had quitted the river in its delicious prison between verdant hills and rocky precipices.' This is the Rhine north of Bingen. This pastoral countryside also contains some of the most romantic castles in the Rhineland. The first, Burg Rheinstein, glowers down at us from its 173-metre peak, trees growing from its once mighty tower, vines climbing its ancient walls. Built around 1260, this is one of the oldest of all the Rhine castles (and it shows its age). Partly restored in the nineteenth century, it houses a rich collection of weapons, hunting trophies and furniture. So does Burg Reichenstein a little further on. Even older than Burg Rheinstein, its ivy-covered walls are set in defensive tiers, the inner guarding the outer, and little turrets peep here and there between the castellated towers.

Soon you reach Trechtingshausen, where a combination of ancient fortresses and waterfalls gives this little spot an atmosphere of wild romanticism. The eleventh-century Burg Sooneck overlooks the town from the north-west. Not quite the medieval stronghold it seems, this fairy-tale castle was imaginatively reconstructed by the kings of Prussia in the nineteenth century, who used it as a hunting-lodge. In the rather forlorn cemetery chapel just outside Trechtingshausen is a thirteenth-century church dedicated to St Clemens.

After Trechtingshausen the road runs through the village of Niederheimbach, where Schloss Hohneck, ruined by the French when they invaded this part of Germany in 1689, was restored in 1865. Today it is one of the seats of the knights templars. Driving past these

A Rhine barge sails serenely past Niederheimbach, a tiny wine village with medieval walls and an eleventh-century church.

wild and sometimes fancifully restored castles, I am continually torn between a desire to look across the Rhine at its picturesque right bank and by the equally pressing need to relish the castles and countryside on this side of the river.

Five kilometres further on Bacharach is a little town of half-timbered houses lying at the mouth of the River Steeg, renowned for its wines and still guarded by the ruins of its twelfth-century Schloss Stahleck. On their destructive rampage of 1689 the French demolished most of this castle too. Well-restored and on a promontory to the left of the town, it is approached through vineyards and little clumps of forest. Like so many others, however, it is best enjoyed from afar. Close to, the trappings of the youth hostel it has now become detract from its charm. Surprisingly, the French troops spared Bacharach's other fortifications, in particular its fourteenth-century walls.

Today you can still enjoy the three fortified gateways set along the Rhine, the Krahntor in the south, the Markttor in the middle and the Münztor to the north. At the foot of the *Schloss* stands a ruined chapel, the Wernerkapelle, one of Bacharach's treasures, the lovely red sandstone tracery of its windows a mute testimony to medieval craftsmanship, everything open to the elements. The Werner in question was a Christian boy, supposedly murdered by Jews in the thirteenth century, and this chapel became a celebrated place of pilgrimage in the often anti-Semitic Middle Ages. Seek out too the thirteenth-century romanesque church of St Peter, its high arches now clasped in strong metal bands. Philologists deny that the name Bacharach derives from the Latin for 'altar of Bacchus', but sipping wine in one of the

town's entrancing old inns one would be forgiven for thinking the scholars wrong.

A Rhine legend tells of a beautiful village maiden here who fell in love with a young knight. He plighted his troth, but then rode off to the wars. The maid rejected all her many other suitors, though many became disconsolate with love for her, wandering miserably in the neighbouring forests. Some killed themselves. The other fair women of Bacharach understandably complained to the archbishop that the maid was taking the hearts of their own menfolk by sorcery. The archbishop, charmed by the maid's gentleness, found her innocent. Since her own lover had never returned, and since her beauty had been responsible for the deaths of many a fine knight, she begged to die herself, but the archbishop insisted that she retired to a convent rather than leave this world. The maid had one last request: to climb the heights above Bacharach and gaze for the last time on the castle of her own knight. She did so, and from the edge of the precipice on which she stood she saw a light barque sailing up the Rhine. In it was her own knight. She gave out such a cry that the sailors looked up and distractedly steered the barque on to the rocks. Seeing her loved one perishing, the maiden herself leapt into the Rhine, and the two died together.

The next village downstream, Oberwesel, is likewise dominated by a castle, but Schloss Schönburg, now a hotel and restaurant, has none of the atmosphere of some of its rivals. Oberwesel itself has much more to offer and no one should simply drive straight through it. Stretching along the curving Rhine, its ancient ramparts punctuated by 16 quaint crenellated towers survive precisely as they stood in the Middle Ages, sheltering equally ancient houses as well as an early fourteenth-century sandstone church dedicated to Our Lady. The golden high altar here is as old as the church, its rood loft some twenty years later, its organ-case baroque. Find, too, the late thirteenth-century church of St Martin, with its beautiful

Wherever you are on the Rhine, the opposite bank boasts villages and castles as romantic as those on your side of the river. This view of St Goarshausen is from near Oberwesel.

135

renaissance pulpit. These two striking buildings are known as the red church and the white church respectively, from the colour of the stone.

Here on an island in the middle of the river stands the lovely Pfalzgrafenstein, a castle which Ludwig the Bavarian built in 1327 to collect river tolls and where he subsequently met Pope John XXII in an attempt to resolve their differences. Here nature and architecture combine to create a scene unrivalled even along the Rhine. The white walls surmounted by pepperpot roofs are set against the greenery of the island and the blue of the river. The pentagonal central tower was built by Ludwig, but the castle was not finished until the seventeenth century, and the whole ensemble is enriched by a late gothic quaintness. It looks as if it might suddenly loose itself from its moorings and sail off down river.

Some 7 kilometres away is the little town of St Goar, named after a sixth-century hermit who came here from Aquitaine in France. His enemies, alarmed at his solitary pattern of life, denounced him to Bishop Rusticus of Trier as a sorcerer and hypocrite. Fortunately the king of Austrasia heard of it, examined Goar at Metz, the capital of his kingdom, proclaimed him innocent and deposed Bishop Rusticus. Goar returned to his cave here and died in peace. His bones used to reside in the romanesque crypt of the fifteenth-century parish church, but they have disappeared.

St Goar is dominated by the ruined fortress of Rheinfels, the largest on the Rhine, well worth the 20-minute climb to reach it. Built by one of the counts of Katzenellenbogen in 1245, it was greatly extended in the 1560s by Philip II, landgrave of Hesse-Rheinfels, and then destroyed by the French in 1797. There are also remnants of the old ramparts – the so-called witches' tower and the chancery tower. And as you walk through the town on the way up to the castle, look for the obelisk which stands against the churchyard wall. It is a copy of a Celtic sacrificial stone, known as the *Flammensäule* – flame column.

Drive on through Hirzenach, with its romanesque church, to Bad Salzig. The thermal waters of this spa are renowned, but if you have neither the time nor the inclination to take them, content yourself with some of the luscious cherries grown around the little town.

Five kilometres later the picturesque town of Boppard marks the great loop in the Rhine known as the Bopparder Hamm, with the village of Spay set in the curve of the meander where the Rhine turns north again. The Bopparder Hamm is perfect south-facing vineyard country. As the Celtic obelisk at St Goar has already indicated, the whole region has been inhabited for many centuries, and the name Boppard derives from the Celtic *Baudobriga*. Next to the municipal museum, which is housed in the former palace of the electors of Trier, are the remains of Roman fortifications. There is also a romanesque parish church, its two slender twelfth-century towers soaring above the market square. And if your taste for churchgoing is strong enough, walk to the railway station to explore the furnishings, wall-paintings and tombs inside the fifteenth-century Carmelite church. Another treat is to take the chair-lift to the Gedeonseck, 305 metres high, for a panorama of the great curve of the river.

These enchanting little towns mislead us by their size, suggesting that nothing of major importance has ever happened in them. But it was at Rhens, reached from Boppard through 12 kilometres of vineyards, that the electors of Germany used to meet to choose their emperor, conveniently positioned as it was where the fiefs of four of the seven electors had a common border. They gathered at what was called the Königstuhl, no doubt glad that the town was fortified – as it still is in part. Twentieth-century tourists might more con-

The holy well of Oberwesel, a village with two beautiful contrasting churches, one white and one red.

veniently gather at the jolly hotel, Zum Königstuhl, on the river bank, after a stroll through streets of half-timbered houses, often beautifully decorated with painted flowers and diaperwork. Do not miss the house of the Teutonic knights and the old gabled town hall looking across the river, a simple building with white walls and timber painted a ruddy brown.

The road has scarcely left Rhens when it reaches Kapellen-Stolzenfels, lying at the foot of the rock which supports the impressive Burg Stolzenfels, 100 metres above the river. This louring fortress glares across at Burg Lahneck, both of them powerful reminders of the uncertainties of life in the past. Burg Stolzenfels was partly ruined by the French in 1689, but in 1823 it came into the hands of a Prussian prince who later became King Friedrich Wilhelm IV. The Berlin architect Karl Friedrich Schinkel helped him to rebuild Burg Stolzenfels in the gothic style. Today it is well worth clambering up to the castle to see its great hall, the chapel, the armoury and the collection of antique furniture. The garden is a delight of rose-festooned pergolas. Burg Stolzenfels is mid nineteenth-century gothicism at its most fanciful, with battlements and crenellations, arches, turrets and waterfalls. For me it works very well. Even more splendid is the view from the peak, with a vista over Koblenz.

This entrancing city is now only 6 kilometres away, magically situated where three great valleys meet and the Moselle flows into the Rhine. Its name derives from the word confluence, originating in a Roman camp set up here in 9 BC called *castrum ad confluentes*. Close by rise the mountainous Taunus, Eifel and Hunsrück. The city's superb strategic position contributed to its importance over many centuries. Imperial diets were held here, and when the three sons of Louis the

The island fortress of Pfalzgrafenstein was built like an elegant stone ship in 1327, with the bastion added in 1607.

Debonair decided to divide his empire amongst themselves in 843, the preliminaries of the famous Treaty of Verdun which codified their agreement were arranged by 110 delegates at Koblenz.

The great buildings of the city reflect the ambitions and wealth of its ecclesiastics as well as its secular princes, the splendour of what stands today indicating what has been lost in the many fierce struggles for the city. During the Thirty Years' War, for instance, Koblenz passed successively into the hands of the French, the Spanish, the Swedes and the forces of the Holy Roman Emperor. Scarcely was that war over when the armies of the Sun King, Louis XIV, destroyed two-thirds of the city in 1688.

The prince-electors of Trier rebuilt Koblenz and made it their home. In 1789 the last of these monarchs, the cultivated, art-loving Clemens-Wenzeslaus, made the error of giving refuge to nobility fleeing the French Revolution. For a time Koblenz was known as 'Little Paris'. Then in 1794 the French General Marceau invaded the electorate, easily defeated the forces of Clemens-Wenzeslaus, and took the city for France.

Marceau was killed in battle two years later, and he is commemorated in a monument which stands just outside the city above Koblenz-Lützel. One of its inscriptions reads: *Hic cineras, ubique nomen* (Here lie the ashes, his name is everywhere). Even the general's enemies acknowledged Marceau's bravery and skill.

By Coblentz, on a rise of gentle ground,
There is a small and simple pyramid,
Crowning the summit of the verdant mound;
Beneath its base are heroes' ashes hid,
Our enemy's – but let that not forbid
Honour to Marceau! o'er whose early tomb
Tears, big tears, gush'd from the rough soldier's lid,
Lamenting and yet envying such a doom,
Falling for France, whose rights he battled to resume.

The words are Byron's.

INDEM
MARIEN

BILTGEN

FA MARIA AB

Above and left **Rhens is a town of half-timbered and gabled houses splendidly restored after the destruction of World War II, many with delightfully decorated oriel windows like this one.**

Left This delightful *trompe-l'oeil* painting decorates the wall of a house in Koblenz.

Above A classical square in Koblenz, a city built on the site of a Roman camp in the Middle Ages and then enhanced in a second golden age, the seventeenth and eighteenth centuries.

143

With the defeat of Napoleon, Koblenz reverted to Germany, and in 1845 received a singular honour: Clemens-Wenzeslaus's former electoral palace became the residence of the future Kaiser Wilhelm I and his bride Augusta. No one should miss an opportunity to see this electoral palace, the Kürfürsliches Schloss. Since the elector for whom it was built was so closely tied to the doomed court of the French King Louis XVI, it comes as no surprise that its architects were two Frenchmen, Pierre-Michel d'Ixnard and Antoine François Peyre. Their palace is the most important example of pure French classicism in the whole Rhine valley, and one of the finest to be found anywhere outside France. Its long, severely classical façade is enriched by a massive portico supported by eight Doric columns. Not far away, in the Neustadt to the left of the palace, stands the city theatre. Another example of Clemens-Wenzeslaus's beneficence, it was built in 1787 one year after the completion of his electoral palace and is fronted by a fountain – yet another testimony to this kindly ruler's care for his people. The monument rising from the fountain is inscribed: 'From Clemens-Wenzeslaus, prince-elector, to his neighbours, 1791'.

If you are in Koblenz when the weather is clement, visit the park on the left bank of the Rhine with its walks sheltered by maples and graced with willows. Open-air concerts and operettas are held here in the summer, the operetta stage actually floating on the river. And then there is the *Weindorf*, a half-timbered wine village created in 1925 at the corner of the Pfaffendorfer bridge, looking for all the world like a legacy of the Middle Ages. You can taste and buy the wines of the Rhine and the Moselle in four typical regional houses set up here.

A stroll north from here along the river bank brings you to the impressive church of St Kastor, its chaste white walls rising from a green garden. St Kastor was founded in 836 but dates for the most part from the end of the twelfth century. This is not the only romanesque church in Koblenz. There are in fact two others: the Liebfrauenkirche and the Florinskirche, and indeed the former's prominent twin bulbous towers have provided Koblenz with its civic emblem. But the Kastorkirche with its four towers is, I think, the finest. And I like the homely clock on the right-hand tower of the mighty west façade, striking a slightly incongruous note against the austerity of the romanesque architecture.

In the middle of this church square is an historical curiosity, the base of a fountain set up in honour of Napoleon during the emperor's disastrous Russian campaign. When the Russian troops subsequently crossed the Rhine at Koblenz, intending to finish off Napoleon once and for all, their own commandant added an inscription in French, 'Seen and approved by us, Russian Commandant of Koblenz, 1 January 1814'.

Go south along the river past the house of the Teutonic knights – or what remains of the headquarters founded here in 1216 – to see Koblenz's celebrated *Deutsches Eck*, the once heavily-fortified corner that juts out at the confluence of the Moselle and the Rhine. Not only have its fortifications largely disappeared, mostly destroyed in 1945, but so too has the massive equestrian statue of Kaiser Wilhelm I set up here in 1897, another casualty of World War II. Only its base remains, ironically inscribed, 'The empire will never be defeated so long as your loyalty remains.' The view from here is breathtaking, especially if you climb the 107 steps up the pedestal. Across the river rises the fortress of Ehrenbreitstein, while along the Moselle to the right you can see the towers and former castle of old Koblenz and the medieval Baldwin's bridge across the river.

Archbishop Baldwin of Luxembourg, brother of the

Koblenz's former Kaufhaus and court, now the middle-Rhine museum, still looks gothic in spite of alterations in the eighteenth century.

Austrian Emperor Heinrich VII, commissioned the Moselle bridge in 1343, and 11 of the original 14 arches still stand. Walk down to the bridge past half-timbered houses lining the river bank and the old *Schloss*, built in the late thirteenth century to guard the river crossing. From half-way along the ancient structure there is one of the finest views of the Moselle that I know.

Like so many great rivers, the waters of the Moselle are curiously distinctive, a fact noticed by Thomas Hood, who visited Koblenz in 1839. For him the Moselle was blue, whereas the mingling of the waters at the Rhine had a greenish tinge. Their junction reminded him of an ill-assorted marriage. 'I could name more than one couple where, like the Rhine and the Moselle, the lady is rather yellow and the gentleman looks blue', was Hood's sardonic comment.

The two great rivers inspired Thomas Hood to write a poem outlining the consequences of an ill-conceived match. He tells the sad tale of a Koblenz woman whose truant husband had been away from home for nine years, two months, a week and half a day without sending his wife a single word. Weary of solitude the woman took two candles into the chapel on the hill known as St Petersberg on the far side of the river and prayed before the Blessed Virgin to be a *bona fide* wife once more:

> Oh holy Virgin! listen to my prayer!
> And for sweet mercy, and thy sex's sake,
> Accept the vows and offerings I make –
> Others set up one light, but here's *a pair!*

The prayer was efficacious. Within three weeks she was standing before the priest with her new husband by her side. At the wedding feast tables groaned and

---

The early seventeenth-century façade of this doorway is all that remains of the original Jesuit church in Koblenz.

everyone was making merry, when, unwelcome and unasked, like Banquo's ghost, the long-lost spouse suddenly walked in.

Hood's moral is this:

> Ye Coblenz maids take warning by the rhyme,
> And as our Christian laws forbid polygamy,
> For fear of bigamy,
> Only light *one* taper at a time.

Sitting in the chapel on St Petersberg (where incidentally there is a monument to General Marceau), Hood mused on the blessed state of the saints in heaven, where none are given in marriage. Nevertheless his description of the marriage feast of the luckless woman shows a true appreciation of the good things in life:

Rich was the Wedding Feast and rare –
> What sausages were there!
Of sweets and sours there was a perfect glut;
With plenteous liquors to wash down good cheer;
Brantwein, and Rhum, Kirsch-wasser, and Krug Bier,
And wine so *sharp* that ev'ry one was *cut.*

Hood's verse could be a recipe for eating and drinking in Koblenz today, except that he neglects to mention the exquisite Moselle wine. The American novelist Herman Melville, who reached Koblenz in 1849, would have agreed. He found a large party assembled at his hotel, each man with his bottle of Rhenish wine and his cigar. Melville chose differently. 'At dinner I drank nothing but Moselle wine', he recorded, thus obeying the maxim 'drink the wine of the country in which you may be travelling'. He judged the Moselle wine to be 'bluish – at least *tinged* with blue', seeming to have been extracted from the waters of the river after which it is named.

Cross the Moselle and drive through the suburb of Lützel to the industrial town of Weissenthurm. The centre of the German breeze-block industry might seem an unpromising spot for historical gems, but this

Groaning men and sweet ladies support the portico of the late sixteenth-century city museum at Andernach.

unprepossessing place conceals a white keep dated 1370 (from which Weissenthurm derives its name) and an obelisk erected in memory of Napoleon's General Hoche. He crossed the Rhine at Weissenthurm, on his way to Russia in 1797, at roughly the same point crossed by Julius Caesar in 55 BC. Hoche died in the Russian campaign and his ashes were brought to this spot from the cemetery of St Petersburg by Marshal Foch and two French generals in 1919. More prosaically, Weissenthurm is also of interest for its many breweries, with a number of local beers to be sampled. Further on, 17 kilometres north of Koblenz, is Andernach, another old town once enclosed by walls where traces of the ramparts and a ruined medieval *Schloss* can still be seen. One of Andernach's fortified

towers is now a youth hostel. Another, the gothic Rhine gate near the point where river cruisers dock, is decorated with figures of bakers' boys.

Andernach is a lovely town to explore. The beautiful romanesque parish church with four towers was begun after a fire in 1198 burned down an earlier building, and finished around 1220. Friezes and carvings decorate its doorways, and inside the vaulting is delicately ogival. Andernach also boasts a fourteenth-century Protestant church and a town hall built two centuries later, with an ancient, deep Jewish ritual bath in its courtyard.

Drive on northwards, past Andernach's sixteenth-century crane, which remained in use until 1911. The route along the river passes through the suburb of Namedy, where there is another thirteenth-century church and a sixteenth-century *Schloss* that was greatly enlarged 300 years later. Eight kilometres beyond Andernach you can make an excursion from the industrial town of Brohl-Lützing to the celebrated monastery of Maria Laach, 'St Mary beside the lake'. This gem lies to the west along the B412 in the volcanic uplands known as the Eifel, beside a vast water-filled crater called Lake Laacher. The lake itself is stunning. Eight kilometres in circumference and in places 53 metres deep, it is surrounded by extinct volcanic cones – no fewer than 31 of them – and has a distinctly eerie atmosphere. The Benedictine abbey church of Maria Laach lies at the south-western end of the lake, an exquisite six-towered romanesque building. Some towers are round, some are square, one is octagonal. Its cool, shady cloisters surround an ancient garden. The count-palatine Heinrich II who founded the monastery in 1093 lies inside its church in a thirteenth-century

A romanesque monastic masterpiece: the abbey church of Maria Laach, begun in 1093, finished around 1220 and entirely harmonious in style.

tomb. The monastery was secularized in 1802, but the monks have returned to Maria Laach and are today equally welcoming to the tourist and dedicated to their daily offices. No one with half a day to spare should miss this memorable place.

Return to Brohl and the Rhine. Less than 4 kilometres north is the spa of Bad Breisig, where you can bathe in a pool filled with the thermal waters. The town is still partly protected by its old fortifications and is overlooked by Schloss Rheineck, high on a 182-metre peak. Half-timbered customs houses front the river, and the town is surrounded by magnificent forests. If you arrive at Bad Breisig in September you may be fortunate enough to enjoy its annual onion market.

Drive on to Sinzig, another old, partly fortified spa town, with a severely beautiful romanesque church. Naturally there is a *Schloss* here too. And there is a memorial to the twelfth-century Holy Roman Emperor Frederick Barbarossa, representing him as some ham actor playing a medieval knight, one armoured leg jutting forward through his robes. If you want to spend an hour or two sunbathing by the riverside, the information office will direct you to a beach stretching gently down to the Rhine. The road north rejoins the river at Remagen, passing the mouth of its tributary the Ahr on the way. Remagen was another Roman camp on the Rhine, but is best known as the place where General Ludendorff ordered the building of a bridge across the river in 1918. During World War II this was the only crossing-point which had not been destroyed and became famous when American troops took and crossed it on 7 March 1945. Ten days later the bridge collapsed. Today the tower of Remagen's railway bridge appropriately houses a peace museum.

From now on the road runs close to the Rhine through Oberwinter to Rolandseck, from where there are splendid views across the river to the Siebengebirge. Why these hills are called mountains I cannot say. I am also not at all sure that there are seven. I have frequently tried to count them from this side of the river and have always failed to reach the right number. Rich, ample and craggy they certainly are, volcanic remnants like the Eifel range. The best known and most climbed is the Drachenfels, with its ruined twelfth-century castle, immortalized by Byron in *Childe Harolde's Pilgrimage*:

> The castled crag of Drachenfels
> Frowns o'er the wide and winding Rhine,
> Whose breast of waters broadly swells
> Between the banks which bear the vine;
> And hills all rich with blossomed trees,
> And fields which promise corn and wine,
> And scattered cities, crowning these,
> Whose fair white walls along them shine . . .

From Rolandseck you can also see the island of Nonnenwerth in the middle of the Rhine, compared by George Meredith to a dewy blushing rose between the two white breasts of a woman we love. The surviving monastic buildings of the nunnery founded here in 1122 are now a girls' school. Of all unsuitably libidinous people, Franz Liszt once lived there.

In 1832 Alfred Tennyson and his friend Arthur Hallam climbed up through the vineyards to the top of the Drachenfels, where they ate cherries and gazed northwards to the unfinished spires of Cologne cathedral. They then clambered down to the river's edge, and engaged a strong peasant woman to row them across to the island of Nonnenwerth. A steamer almost ran them down on the way. Hallam tried to make the woman change course, but happily she refused for (as Tennyson realized) Hallam's advice would surely have taken them directly under the steamer's bows. At Nonnenwerth the two men lodged at a decent hotel in the former convent and marvelled at the splendid view of the Siebengebirge.

Winter melancholy outside Brohl-Lützing.

The road now crosses into the region of Germany known as Rhineland-Palatinate and passes through the huge suburb of Bad Godesberg, home of most of the diplomats accredited to the West German government at Bonn. At least seventy embassies are situated here. Diplomats, sent, as Francis Bacon put it, 'to lie in a foreign country' at the expense of their own country's taxpayers, are cultivated men and women and usually choose to live in agreeable surroundings. With its beautiful villas, lovely gardens, thermal waters reputed in Roman times, and a fine view of the Siebengebirge, Bad Godesberg is no exception. The waters are said to cure biliousness, thus no doubt smoothing the sometimes heated machinations of diplomacy. This is where Neville Chamberlain came in 1938 and was so softened up by Adolf Hitler's rages that he soon agreed that the Nazi chancellor should be allowed to annex the Sudetenland region of Czechoslovakia.

The magnificent Kurpark here does calm one's spirits. The Kurhaus-Redouté, dating from 1791, offers full-scale concerts and chamber music in its Beethoven hall. I find the ironwork of the park railing even more delightful than the Redouté itself. To the west of the town on a peak 122 metres above the river stands the former palace of the Elector of Cologne, Burg Godesburg, a powerful, louring fortress partly ruined by Bavarian troops in 1583 and now transformed into a splendid hotel and restaurant.

The diplomats of Bad Godesberg have an 8-kilometre journey to work in Bonn, capital of the Federal Republic of Germany. Ludwig van Beethoven was born here in 1770, and the modest house in which he came into the world is now a Beethoven museum. Of all the mementoes of the great man displayed here, I am

A musical reminder that Bonn is the birthplace of Beethoven and that Robert and Clara Schumann as well as Wagner's great love Mathilde Wesendonck rest in the old cemetery.

most touched by the devices with which the composer sought to alleviate his increasing deafness. And the little house contrasts strikingly with the massive Beethovenhalle built just north of the Kennedy bridge in the 1950s. Other poignant musical memorials can be seen in the old cemetery, where Robert Schumann and his wife as well as Beethoven's mother lie buried. A pretty and studious cherub endlessly plays the violin on Schumann's monument.

The heart of old Bonn is its triangular market-place, flanked by the fifteenth-century church of St Remigius and the eighteenth-century baroque town hall, with its elegant exterior staircase. If the church of St Remigius is fine, Bonn's minster is one of the best

Ernst Hähnel's monumental statue of Beethoven turns its back on the post office in Bonn's Münsterplatz.

romanesque churches of the Rhine valley. Its exquisite cloisters date from 1126 to 1169, when the artistically inspired prior Gerhard d'Arc commissioned skilled craftsmen to enhance his collegiate church. And do not leave the town without seeking out the main building of Bonn university, once the palace of the prince-electors of Cologne and designed by Robert de Cotte and Enrico Zucalli between 1697 and 1725. It seems this magnificent building did not satisfy the prince-electors, as they then engaged de Cotte to build them a summer palace as well. Schloss Poppelsdorf was completed in 1745 and looks out over an entrancing botanical garden.

In ten minutes' walk from this *Schloss* you can reach the top of the Kreuzberg, where a fine church that was once part of a Franciscan monastery has been a place of pilgrimage since the seventeenth century. Twentieth-century architectural pilgrims will climb up to it to see the baroque chapel with a great marble 'Scala Sancta' – a replica of the staircase Jesus is reputed to have climbed at his trial – created by Balthasar Neumann.

From Bonn a long attractive ridge, the Vorgebirge, runs almost as far as Cologne. South-west of the city on the edge of these fertile hills lies Brühl, at one time part of the lands ruled by the great prince-electors of Cologne. Here one of the most magnificent of these men, Clemens August, commissioned Johann Konrad Schlaun in 1725 to begin work on another summer residence, the magical rococo Schloss Augustusburg.

A delicious rococo detail at Bonn.

The Belgian architect François Cuvilliés continued Schlaun's work, and Balthasar Neumann created a monumental stairwell (as well as a high altar for Brühl's old gothic church). The flower-beds of the park are also laid out in the rococo style, their design worked out by a French gardener named Dominique Girard. An avenue leads from the *Schloss* through the park to a hunting-lodge known as Falkenlust, another beautiful creation by François Cuvilliés.

The town of Brühl lies only 15 kilometres from the archbishops' cathedral at Cologne, and there my next chapter begins.

Bonn's sumptuous town hall, designed by Michael Levilly in the early eighteenth century, one of many elegant buildings adorning the capital of the German Federal Republic.

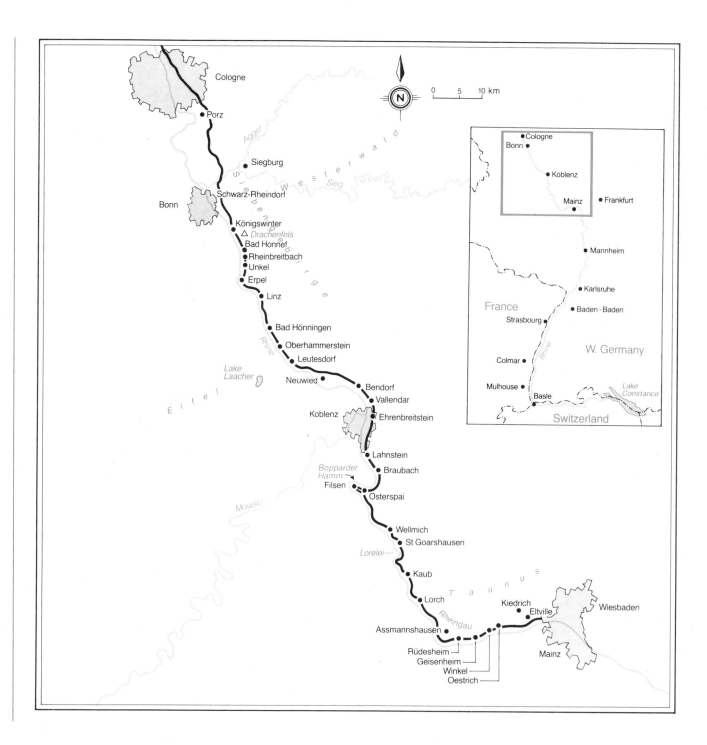

5
Relics,
Sirens and Dragon's Blood

Cologne – Königswinter – Bad Honnef – Unkel –
Linz – Bad Hönningen – Neuwied – Bendorf –
Lahnstein – St Goarshausen – Kaub – Lorch –
Rüdesheim – Geisenheim – Winkel –
Kloster Eberbach – Eltville

Long before I visited the city I had seen Cologne frequently from the railway, and I hope to do so many times again. The massive German locomotives slowly pull your carriage across the Hohenzollern bridge high above the Rhine. Gabled houses with painted façades shadowed by the towers of the church of Great St Martin and the mighty spires of the cathedral loom ahead. The train stops at Cologne's *Hauptbahnhof*, scarcely 200 metres from the cathedral itself. With a wisdom unusual in town planners, the architects of the station have made the wall looking on to the cathedral a huge sheet of glass, so you can view the masterpiece without fear of missing your train. For me the temptation has often been more than I can resist. Time and time again I have run from the railway train, leaving my baggage perilously behind, to exult over the massive building at closer quarters. Then I have run back again and leapt into my carriage just as the locomotive was hissing its way out of Cologne and heading north.

Thus for me Cologne was fraught with excitement and hung around with memories long before I ever stayed there. I was first invited to visit the city in 1982 when the German writers' union was hosting a conference with the city council on the theme of

'writers for peace'. I was at that time working on a biography of Adolf Hitler's courageous German opponent, Martin Niemöller, a former U-boat commander who had survived eight years in Nazi concentration camps and ended his days as a nuclear disarmer. In between each seminar at the conference, smiling Japanese gently offered everyone pamphlets and poems deploring the atomic destruction of Hiroshima and Nagasaki. Distinguished Russian dissidents and a few non-dissidents read their works. As an Englishman I was unjustly upbraided for my supposed complicity in the recent British fracas over the Falkland Islands. We assembled scribes were told that the role of the writer in society was to 'Do what is useless; sing the songs no one expects you to sing! Make trouble; be a spanner in the works and not the oil that oils the world's wheels.' I agreed, not quite sure, however, how to achieve this dissidence. More speeches followed, seeming to embrace every global issue.

Soon I slipped quietly away, back to the Hotel Königshof where I had earlier eaten a hearty Cologne breakfast which included several kinds of sausage, salads and sliced black pudding. It was then I realized for the first time that the Hotel Königshof is just

around the corner from Cologne cathedral. The sun was shining, and after a first look inside the cathedral I made my way to the Hohenzollern bridge which I had so often crossed in a railway carriage. Standing in the middle of it, dizzily rocked by the powerful trains passing by, I gazed back at the waterfront dominated by the towers of the city's medieval masterpiece while the river flowed powerfully below.

That was the start of my love affair with Cologne, a city which I had previously foolishly supposed to be boring because of its almost total destruction during World War II. Remarkably, the desolation produced by the allied bombs is now something the citizens of Cologne can joke about. The two legendary Cologne characters known as Tönnes and Schael (the Mick and Pat of the Rhineland) are said to have met just after that war ended. Tönnes asked Schael where he was living. Schael replied, 'In the nearest house to the cathedral, about 18 kilometres away'. In between there was nothing but rubble.

Many others have experienced a similar love affair with the River Rhine in the stretch from Cologne upstream to the wine village of Rüdesheim. This is the landscape of a thousand fairy-tales, with castle-crowned crags rising precipitously from the river, as if part of a vast set for a new film version of *Camelot*. The powerful emotional response to such picturesque beauty is almost impossible to put into words, although Byron perhaps came close to describing the enchantment that every visitor feels:

Above, the frequent feudal towers
Through green leaves lift their walls of gray;
And many a rock which steeply lowers,
And noble arch in proud decay,
Look o'er this vale of vintage-bowers . . .

The best-known spires in Germany: Cologne cathedral by night.

The river nobly foams and flows;
The charm of this enchanted ground,
And all its thousand turns disclose
Some fresher beauty, varying round:
The haughtiest breast its wish might bound
Through life to dwell delighted here;
Nor could on earth a spot be found
To nature and to me so dear.

Cologne is where most visitors to the Rhine have begun their tour. 'In this antiquated gable-ended old town – full of Middle Age, Charlemagne associations – where Rubens was born and Mary de Medici died, there is much to interest a pondering man like me,' wrote Herman Melville in 1849. Melville roamed about the city, looking at the churches, buying cigars off pretty girls and stopping people in the street to ask for a light. 'I drank in the very vital spirit and soul of old Charlemagne, as I turned the quaint old corners of this quaint old town.'

Since then war has changed the face of the city. The 'labyrinth of little streets' enjoyed by the novelist Alexandre Dumas in the nineteenth century disappeared in World War II. Allied bombs destroyed 90 per cent of inner Cologne and 70 per cent of the suburbs, but miraculously they did not demolish the great cathedral. Although 14 of them scored direct hits on the stupendous gothic building, it survived them all.

Cologne cathedral took all of 632 years to complete. None the less, architecturally it is a perfectly harmonious whole, basically pure high gothic. Could Archbishop Konrad von Hochstaufen, who laid its foundation stone in 1248, have possibly conceived that three hundred years later building would have come to a standstill, his cathedral still half-finished? Four hundred years on Thomas Hood described the still truncated church as 'an uncomfortable sight' and 'a broken promise to God'.

Scarcely anyone believed it would ever be

completed. Nineteenth-century visitors were both entranced and made miserable by its unfinished state. William Wordsworth summoned all his powers to call for divine help to finish the mighty building. Its gothic vastness appealed to his sense of the sublime; its very incompleteness to his panthistic belief in supernatural powers:

> O for the help of Angels to complete
> This Temple – Angels governed by a plan
> Thus far pursued (how gloriously!) by Man.

Then came signs of hope. A crane appeared high up on the west end. 'Sailed out before breakfast and found my way to the famous cathedral, where the everlasting ''crane'' stands on the tower', wrote Melville. Work was at last progressing. Herman Melville observed how the new stone of one nearly completed transept contrasted strangely with the ruinous condition of the vast unfinished tower.

The crane in question was employed after 1842, when work on the original plan of the building was resumed, and it continued to lift stone to the top of the tower until 1868. By 1880 Cologne cathedral was finished. It embodied everything that the nineteenth century and I love in a great church. Lewis Carroll rightly dubbed it 'the most beautiful of all the churches I have ever seen or can imagine'. He added, 'If one could imagine the spirit of devotion embodied in any material form, it would be in such a building.'

The most obvious reason for this absurd delay in finishing Cologne cathedral is that it is huge. No other church in the world has a façade so vast. Until the Eiffel Tower was constructed in 1889 the two west towers of the cathedral, each over 153 metres high, were taller than any other building in western Europe. As you gaze up from below, the finials on top of each tower appear to be tiny. Look at the full-size replica of one of them in the cathedral square. It stands a solid 9.25 metres high and 4.58 metres wide. If you have the stamina, you can climb one of the towers for a stunning panorama of the city itself, or over the wide River Rhine to the peaks of the Siebengebirge to the south and the hills of the Bergisches Land to the east.

Then go inside for a breathtaking experience. Borne on 56 pillars, the vault of Cologne cathedral soars sublimely above the visitors clustered below. The choir remains virtually as it was when it was first built. Fourteen pillars bear statues of Jesus and his apostles, carved in around 1320. At the same time artists were decorating the walls of the choir with delicate paintings that have survived the vicissitudes of the centuries – quite remarkably in view of the fact that the French converted the unfinished building into a barn in 1796, filled it with hay and stripped the lead from its roof. Most of the exquisite stained glass in the choir and its surrounding chapels dates from the early thirteenth century. As for the medieval choir-stalls, as one would expect in this huge cathedral church, they are the largest in Christendom. Two of their seats are reserved for the pope and the Holy Roman Emperor.

This stupendous building houses three extraordinary relics, the skulls of the Magi, those legendary kings who came from the east with gifts for the infant Jesus. Each monarch's name is emblazoned on his skull in rubies: Caspar, Melchior, Balthazar. The authorities sometimes put jewelled crowns on the three saintly heads. On special feast days part of the shrine is opened, and they are exposed to view and for people to touch. Helen, the mother of the Roman Emperor Constantine (?285–337), is said to have discovered this spiritual treasure-trove on her visit to the Holy Land and to have sent the relics back to Constantinople. In the sixth century they were transferred to the church of St Eustorgio, Milan, where they remained till 1164, when the Emperor Frederick Barbarossa attacked and defeated the city. He plundered the holy skulls and

The busy portal of Cologne cathedral, perhaps the most impressive gothic church in Europe.

gave them to his chaplain, who was Archbishop of Cologne.

Today they reside in an exquisite golden shrine, one of the masterpieces of early thirteenth-century craftsmanship. Many others have worked on this shrine over the centuries, but its beauty derives from the skill of the brilliant Nicholas of Verdun. A word of high praise is also due to a twentieth-century goldsmith named Peter Bolg, who in 1973 repaired the damage done to the shrine during World War II. In the same year the Archbishop of Cologne generously gave a fragment of the Magi's skulls back to the church of St Eustorgio, Milan. The relics have lost none of their appeal. In 1974, when the new shrine and its dusty bones were venerated at the feast of the Epiphany, 20,000 pilgrims crowded into Cologne cathedral to see them. The following year the number visiting the shrine of the Magi during the same feast had swelled to 100,000. Although these figures seem scarcely credible, the cathedral is visited by 17,000 people daily.

And these are not the only holy bones you can see in Cologne. Before the city had a proper sewage system, the romantic poet Samuel Taylor Coleridge summed it up as a city of stenches and stinks, monks and bones:

> The River Rhine, it is well known,
> Doth wash your city of Cologne;
> But tell me Nymphs, what power divine
> Shall henceforth wash the River Rhine?

Today the stenches have gone, but the bones remain in abundance. A beautiful church close by the cathedral not only possesses the skull of a British queen, St Ursula, but also bits of her 11,000 companions. Legend has it that a fierce pagan tyrant coveted Ursula's hand in marriage. She consented to marry him on condition that he converted to Christianity and also allowed her and her 11,000 maiden companions to sail on a pilgrimage. This he did, and by way of Cologne they journeyed on to Rome, where they met the pope. On their return journey they were less fortunate, and were all massacred by the Huns in 238.

These women were buried in the Roman cemetery which is now the site of St Ursula's church. An ancient stone let into the wall of the present building records that a certain Clematius built a church over the virgin martyrs' grave in the fourth century. This was forgotten until excavators began digging the foundations of a new city wall in 1106, when they accidentally dug up the saintly bones. The city rejoiced. Soon countless more saintly bones were excavated – as Byron wonderingly put it:

> Eleven thousand maidenheads of bone:
> The greatest number flesh has ever known.

It is worth visiting St Ursula's church not only because it is a beautiful romanesque building but also to see its so-called Golden Chamber, a chapel built on the south side in the seventeenth century. Here thousands and thousands of bones, all deemed to come from the skeletons of saints, are arranged in brilliantly inventive patterns, protected by wire netting. Rows of shelves below these relics carry reliquary busts, encasing the heads of other saints. A glass container on the altar holds what is reputed to be the head of Queen Ursula herself.

As well as St Ursula's, Cologne possesses no fewer than eleven other majestic romanesque churches. Although all were partly destroyed by the Allies in World War II, the Germans have doggedly restored them in faithful detail. Not all are used for religious worship. St Aposteln, for instance, is a splendid concert hall. When I attended the official celebrations to mark the completion of the restoration of the romanesque churches, the official tour began at St Aposteln with coffee and a glass or two of schnapps – an excellent way of demonstrating that a church has been secularized.

The diamond-shaped spire of St Aposteln dominates the bustling Neumarkt, where market stalls sell

The peasant goes to war; a rustic scene in Cologne.

everything from fruit and wool to Cologne beer. Nearby is Gonski's bookshop, a haven for bibliophiles, while the Schnütgen museum of medieval art across the road is packed with ivories, gothic sculpture and stained glass, some of which spills over into the twelfth-century church of St Cecilia next door. As Christmas approaches, the Neumarkt becomes yet more entrancing. Throughout December it is transformed into a cornucopia of Christmas presents. Festive with Christmas trees and gaily lit after dark, the market is invaded by handloom weavers, and St Aposteln is filled for Christmas concerts.

Much of the centre of Cologne is pedestrianized, and you can cross the heart of the city in twenty minutes or so. Hohestrasse, an animated street of bars, boutiques and restaurants as well as large department stores, exactly traces the route of the Roman road which bisected the city two thousand years ago. Few shoppers can resist buying some of the renowned eau-de-Cologne, a perfume invented by an Italian chemist named Giovanni Maria Farina who came to live here in 1709. Now millions of litres are produced every week. In the years when the city stank horribly, many visitors found the contrast piquant, wondering how such a pungently smelly city could produce such a delicate scent:

> The old Catholic city was still,
> In the Minster the vespers were sung,
> And, re-echoed in cadences shrill,
> The last call of trumpet had rung:
> While across the broad stream of the Rhine,
> The full Moon cast a silvery zone;
> And, methought, as I gazed on its shine,
> 'Surely, that is the Eau de Cologne',

wrote Thomas Hood, addressing a flask of Rhine water. Then the perfume reminded him of his beloved lady and he banished all curmudgeonly thoughts.

> I inquired not the place of its source,
> If it ran to the east or the west;
> But my heart took a note of its course,
> That it flowed towards Her I love best –
> That it flowed towards Her I love best,
> Like those wandering thoughts of my own,
> And the fancy such sweetness possess'd,
> That the Rhine seemed all Eau de Cologne!

Architecturally modern Cologne sometimes clashes violently with its medieval remains, and the citizens themselves had heated arguments when it was decided to build the ultra-modernistic Wallraf-Richartz museum directly between the great cathedral and the Rheingarten on the river bank. I am on the side of the objectors. That said, I never fail to visit the museum's fantastic art collection on a trip to the city. My two favourite pictures are Stefan Lochner's *Last Judgment* and Otto Dix's portrait of a doctor. Both are macabre.

Lochner, who died in 1451, was Cologne's greatest medieval artist. His *Last Judgment*, illustrating the vanity of riches, depicts a devil carrying off a terrified fat man who still clutches his useless bursting moneybags. The professions of those entering the jaws of hell are identified by their hats – a bishop's mitre, a papal tiara and so on – while the saved rise to a heaven which is exactly like Cologne cathedral. As for Otto Dix's scarfaced doctor, painted over five centuries later, he stands surrounded by all sorts of fearsome, evil-looking instruments: rubber pipes, syringes, nasty potions and surgical knives.

Walk down to the Rhine past the splendid town hall. Its early fifteenth-century belfry and its ravishing renaissance loggia were both badly damaged during the war and both have been beautifully restored. The new part now displays Roman remains uncovered during the reconstruction, as well as a stern portrait of Konrad Adenauer, Oberbürgermeister of Cologne from 1917 to 1933, opponent of Adolf Hitler, and Federal Germany's redoubtable post-war chancellor.

Ahead you see the powerful crossing tower of another of the city's twelve romanesque churches. This is Great St Martin, built in the twelfth and early thirteenth centuries, reached across a flourishing old market square and fronted by a pillar topped by a statue of St Martin himself, slicing his cloak in two and giving half to a scrawny naked beggar. Cologne's old street pattern has been carefully preserved in this part of the city. Little alleyways lead enticingly between pink and cream houses with pointed roofs and gables – some of them four hundred years old.

With Italian, Chinese and even Argentinian restaurants as well as German establishments, this is the quarter where I would always choose to eat. As I discovered to my cost when I first visited the city, the German cuisine features a variety of substantial snacks with extremely misleading names. Cologne Caviar (*Kölsch Kaviar*), for instance, has nothing to do with sturgeon but consists of a rye bread roll filled with raw onion rings, smoked black pudding and mustard. *Halver Hahn* does not mean half a chicken, but mature Dutch cheese served on rye bread with butter and mustard. My favourite Cologne dish also has the oddest name, *Himmel und Äd*, which means Heaven and Earth. *Himmel und Äd* consists of stewed apples and boiled potatoes, mashed together and topped with a slice of hot black pudding and a dollop of lard.

You can of course eat *haute cuisine* in delectable surroundings in Cologne. One of its most remarkable restaurants, the Bastei, is built on the river bank on the site of an old Prussian bastion. After the Prussians had destroyed the city's defences in the late nineteenth century, they stored an enormous spiked iron railing in this bastion. Their plan was to unroll it along the river front in time of war, so as to stop anyone taking the left bank of the Rhine. By 1920 the bastion had fallen into disrepair. The celebrated Expressionist architect Wilhelm Riphahn dreamed of creating a modernistic restaurant on top of it. By 1924 his dream had come true. He built a temple of glass topped by a small pyramid, part of it supported on a frame stretching 8 metres over the Rhine. For over 25 years the cuisine at the Restaurant Bastei was in the charge of one chef, Herr Gerhard Dillner, who once explained to me the origins of a favourite recipe, *Kalbsmédallion Horscher*. This succulent dish – tender pieces of veal garnished with a purée of mushrooms, served on a base of truffled artichokes and accompanied with slices of goose liver and a sauce Béarnaise – was invented by a famous Madrid restaurateur called Horscher who emigrated to Berlin and opened a restaurant there.

Like most visitors not used to German cuisine, I can eat only one such course. Others have more stamina. Looking out on to the Rhine as he dined, Herman Melville recorded, 'a regular German dinner, and a good one'. After innumerable dishes, which included

Light-hearted clockwork at Cologne.

an apple pudding served between the meat and poultry courses, he drank some capital yellow Rhenish wine. My own preference would be to wash down *Himmel und Äd* with the light beer known as Kölsch. Kölsch is a most useful word, as it can also be used to refer to the Cologne way of life and to the Cologne dialect. Kölsch beer is drunk from tall thin glasses, and the citizens here consume more than a thousand million glasses every year.

In the Buttermarkt, half-way between Hohestrasse and the river, is an invariably crowded night-spot known as 'Papa Joe's Jazz Lokal', where traditional New Orleans jazz is played and gallons of Kölsch are served and consumed. Here a Cologne native once told me, 'It cannot harm you. We prescribe Kölsch in hospitals to wash through people's kidneys. Cologne beer is pure medicine.'

Drive south from Cologne along the right bank of the Rhine through the industrial suburb of Porz. This is scarcely a romantic spot these days, but it does boast an eighteenth-century *Schloss*, surrounded by a moat which I am sure survives from the defences of a much earlier building. I like the art nouveau church in the high street, and the fine view of Cologne across the Severins bridge (an impressive piece of engineering, supported only by one off-centre pillar).

Soon you reach the mouth of one of the Rhine's tributaries, usually crowded with boats and canoes. This is the River Sieg, flowing from the delicious country of the Westerwald, where holiday homes and tourist resorts proliferate. Take the time to visit the best known of these centres, Siegburg, some 10 kilometres east, for it is here that Archbishop Anno of Cologne founded a Benedictine monastery in 1066, perched high up above the confluence of the Sieg and the River Agger, on the peak known as the Michaelsberg. The crypt of the abbey church is still intact. Anno himself lies in one of the numerous rich reliquaries inside the thirteenth-century parish church in the town.

Only a kilometre or so across the mouth of the Sieg lies Schwarz-Rheindorf, with its very beautiful and most unusual two-storey romanesque church. Built between 1151 and 1173, this unique building has both a lower and an upper nave. Nobody seems to know how the church came to be built in this way, though there are numerous theories. Charlemagne's own early ninth-century double chapel at Aix-la-Chapelle might conceivably have set a precedent which was copied by the architect. Another suggestion is that the church at Schwarz-Rheindorf was devised in this way because it was once attached to a convent. The two naves would have allowed the nuns to participate in divine service without being themselves observed by the rest of the congregation. The lower nave contains some inspired frescoes, painted almost as soon as this part of the church was built. Their iconography is subtle, for the artist set about depicting the life and passion of Jesus not so much as these events took place but as they were supposedly foreseen by the prophet Ezekiel. On the south and west sides of the church Ezekiel and the New Testament are painted, so to speak, confronting each other. However, there is no need to be able to understand what these ancient wall-paintings show in order to relish the glowing colours – delicate blues, deep reds, fiery golds and rich oranges – still fresh after almost 800 years. The church also contains the tomb of Archbishop Arnold of Wied, who died in 1156 only four years after consecrating it. Wander round the pretty garden which now surrounds the church to see the charming gallery of little round arches decorating the east side and the apse.

The route now runs picturesquely south-east along the right bank of the river, with views of Bonn rising on the other side of the water. A few kilometres further on you come to one of the finest stretches of mountain scenery along the Rhine, the breathtakingly romantic range of volcanic hills known as the Siebengebirge. Legend has it that these sharp peaks are the spoil-heaps created by giants who dug the channel for the Rhine long ago. Reality is almost as romantic; the Siebengebirge are volcanic, formed from an outpouring of lava some 20 million years ago. Stone from these mountains was used to build Cologne cathedral and the great romanesque churches of the city.

As you drive on to Königswinter, the forests on the slopes of the Petersberg – an outcrop of the Siebengebirge – rise to your left. Königswinter itself is set at the foot of the Drachenfels (the dragon's crag) and is the best place to begin a tour of the Siebengebirge, although it tends to become very crowded in the summer months. This is one of Germany's most popular tourist spots, and demand naturally sends up prices. Thomas Hood found the citizens of this area of Germany rapacious. He resented having to pay good money to see the dusty skulls of the Magi in Cologne. And was it the price of Königswinter hotels that inspired him to write an entertaining doggerel poem warning other visitors of the problem?

Ye Tourists and Travellers, bound to the Rhine,
Provided with passport, that requisite docket,
First listen to one little whisper of mine –
Take care of your pocket! – take care of your pocket!
Old castles you'll see on the vine-covered hill, –
Fine ruins to rivet the eye in its socket –
Once haunts of Baronial Banditti, – and still
Take care of your pocket! – take care of your pocket!

That said, Königswinter caters well for its visitors. The high street is lined with fine late seventeenth- and eighteenth-century houses, built after a fire in 1689 destroyed the old town. One of them, a baroque house of 1732, houses the Siebengebirge museum. The town is also the starting-point for magnificent mountain walks, while the less agile can take advantage of a rack-and-pinion railway to reach a rocky platform only some 35 metres below the summit of the Drachenfels. Constructed in 1853, this rack railway is the oldest in Germany, and rises more than 250 metres over a distance of 1250 metres. The steepest gradient is a dizzy 1:5. The line crosses a viaduct giving a magical view of the Drachenfels, and you can get out on the way up to see the elaborately gothic Schloss Drachenburg, one of the superb mock medieval castles built along the Rhine in the nineteenth century.

Scarcely five minutes' walk up from the terrace of the Drachenfels brings you to the ruins of Burg Drachenfels, all that remains of the fortress built here by Archbishop Arnold of Cologne in the early twelfth century. The castle was already half ruined by the time the Swedes occupied it during the Thirty Years' War, and was then besieged and taken by the Elector of Cologne, Duke Ferdinand of Bavaria, who virtually completed its demolition. Bare stretches of ruined wall now crown the wooded height like jagged teeth. Standing here I wonder if those who once garrisoned the castle ever appreciated the magnificent views east over the peaks of the Siebengebirge (there are some thirty altogether), north as far as Cologne and across the Rhine to the ruins of Schloss Rolandseck, as well as south to many of the towns and villages we shall soon visit: Bad Honnef, Unkel and Erpel. Return to the Drachenfels terrace and take the path running right from the one that comes up from Königswinter, which will lead you to the summit of another peak in the Siebengebirge, the 454-metre Grosser Ölberg.

The Drachenfels crag is named after the dragon slain by Siegfried, the hero of the *Nibelungenlied*, which is said to have made its home in a cavern (the *Drachenloch*) half-way up this hill. Having destroyed the monster, Siegfried washed himself in the dragon's blood to become invulnerable. Today the red wine produced from the sheltered vineyards clustered around the crag is gruesomely known as dragon's blood.

The next village along the Rhine is Rhöndorf, where the doughty German chancellor Konrad Adenauer once lived. He is buried in the local cemetery, and his former home is now a museum dedicated to his long life. Standing among the half-timbered houses

surrounding the early eighteenth-century Chapel of Our Lady, you can see why the one-time Oberbürgermeister of Cologne chose to live here. Today the southern edge of Rhöndorf merges indistinguishably with the spa of Bad Honnef, which nestles between the peaks of the Drachenfels and the Rolandsbogen. Naturally the thermal spring here is called the Dragon's spring. As is usual with such springs, the thermal properties of the alkaline water seem to be able to cure an immense number of ailments, from bad hearts to indigestion. Those seeking a relief from the stresses of everyday life are also undoubtedly helped by the climate, which is warmer than anywhere else in the middle Rhine valley. The gardens of the spa boast a pretty bandstand, and the town's market square is graced by a stunning three-aisled late gothic church.

From Bad Honnef you can visit the 455-metre Löwenberg, with the ruins of a thirteenth-century *Schloss* at the summit. You can also cross to the island in the Rhine known as the Grafenwerth, where I once spent a hot June afternoon by the side of the open-air swimming-pool.

Scarcely 3 kilometres from Bad Honnef is another little wine village, Rheinbreitbach, charmingly situated at the entrance to an expansive valley. A plaque on the wall of the Rheinbreitbacher Hof informs visitors that the brothers Jakob and Wilhelm Grimm lived here in the early nineteenth century while they were writing their celebrated collection of folk and fairy-tales – though some would argue they are more accurately described as horror stories – and it is easy to believe that they derived inspiration from the half-timbered houses and the late medieval castle. Rheinbreitbach's romantic charm is typical of a string of little villages along the route here, such as Unkel, Erpel and Linz, all of them boasting half-timbered houses, some of which will have been painted with idealized pastoral landscapes or clinging vines, all of them offering superb views of the Rhine and the basalt peaks that rise from its valley. And yet each place is also distinctive. Erpel lies at the foot of a cliff rising steeply from the river. Linz, a centre of stone-quarrying, is still partly fortified, and some interesting buildings include a late gothic town hall and a late romanesque church. The Kaisersberg high up above the town is crowned with a *Schloss* built in 1365 and a gothic pilgrimage chapel.

The thermal waters that flow from the Siebengebirge also supply the springs of Bad Hönningen, which lies 6 kilometres south-east of Linz. Not content with its own castle, Bad Hönningen also offers a splendid

Left **Near Bad Honnef.**

Right **An old lady eternally sells bread in the market place at Linz, one of several squares in this town shaded by overhanging half-timbered houses and glorious churches.**

Above **The wine town of Leutesdorf, with its fourteenth-century church and half-timbered houses, stretches leisurely along the river.**

Left **Vineyards wait for spring outside Bad Hönningen, a charming spa on the edge of the Rhine-Westerwald natural park.**

view of Schloss Rheineck (see p.151). I was lucky enough to stay here during the annual wine festival, a feature of most towns and villages in this region. Driving on with a slight hangover the following morning I perked up when I discovered some 3 kilometres further on that the thermal springs at Rheinbrohl are dedicated to the Three Kings of Cologne, no doubt to add the Magi's miraculous powers to the healing properties of the waters. The B42 now runs through stunning scenery to another exquisite village, Oberhammerstein, lying at the foot of a great peak which supports the inevitable battlemented ruin. More interesting than some, this tenth-century castle is where the Holy Roman Emperor Heinrich IV took refuge in 1105, fleeing from his own son who deposed him the following year.

Leutesdorf is rather larger than Oberhammerstein but is similarly devoted to the cultivation of the grape. Pause here if you can to see the lovely baroque altar in the pilgrimage church of St Cross. Then drive on south-east for 7 kilometres to Neuwied, an industrial town which conceals a fine eighteenth-century *Schloss* set in a cool park that is well worth visiting. All those interested in the architecture of this period and its delicate stucco-work should also seek out the still partly fortified suburb of Neuwied-Engers, where half-timbered houses and a chapel set up in thanksgiving by those who escaped a plague in 1662 surround another exquisite baroque building. Built in 1759, it boasts one of those fashionable halls of mirrors inspired by Versailles.

Bendorf 9 kilometres further on is also not immediately attractive, but the suburb of Sayn has a wealth of medieval remains: a thirteenth-century abbey built by Premonstratensian monks; the parish church of St Madardus, built in 1204 (with a set of mechanically operated bells ringing out hymn tunes); and the remains of yet another romantic fortress. Drive on through Vallendar, a largish town with views west across the island of Niederwerth – where there are the remains of a monastery built just before the Reformation – to Koblenz and the *Deutsches Eck* (see p.144), the confluence of the Moselle and the Rhine. Some 5 kilometres further on the road passes the mighty fortress of Ehrenbreitstein, which guarded what was an important Rhine crossing in the Middle Ages. Massively picturesque and splendidly restored – 'a magnificent object truly', as Herman Melville rightly put it – it is now a youth hostel. Even the church of Ehrenbreitstein is fortified, showing the strategic value of this site and the vulnerability of those who lived here. In the eighteenth century life for a moment seemed less precarious, and the citizens employed the baroque genius Balthasar Neumann to build them their gay town hall, a direct contrast with the formidable *Schloss*.

The first fortress on the site of Schloss Ehrenbreit-stein was built by a knight named Heribert, and his work was then expanded by the archbishops of Trier. The French demolished much of the castle in 1801, and it was rebuilt by the Prussian General von Aster between 1816 and 1826. Herman Melville found it 'curious that the finest wine of all the Rhine is grown

right under the guns of Ehrenbreitstein'.

Six kilometres further on there is another example of the medieval need for strongholds. A mountain named after all the saints, the Allerheiligenberg, is crowned by Schloss Lahneck, an originally medieval castle which was despoiled by the French in 1689 and restored in the nineteenth century. The medieval lords of the little town of Lahnstein at the foot of the mountain evidently felt that the protection of Schloss Lahneck was not enough, because they also built Schloss Martineck in the thirteenth century. There are also two romanesque churches here, St Johannes and St Martin, although the interior of St Martin is riotously baroque. St Johannes is comically delightful. The prim square tower with three ascending rows of lights is attached to a simple country church that no one has yet bothered to finish properly. The centre of Lahnstein is a busy market square with a renaissance fountain and a gothic town hall. What a treat such town halls are! Here the rough stone lower storey with slender arched windows is surmounted by elegantly timbered gables. One is topped by a quaint little bell-tower.

At Braubach to the south the road starts to rise, passing a pretty gothic chapel filled with statues yet again dedicated to St Martin – why was the saint so popular in this region? Visit the powerful Schloss Marksburg here, with a square keep set in a triangular courtyard, perched on a rock 150 metres above the river. Surprisingly, the rather grim fortifications shelter much gentler gothic living quarters. The Marksburg takes its name from the chapel dedicated to the Evangelist St Mark built in the *Schloss* in 1437 by Count Philip of Katzenellenbogen. If you are here on the first Sunday in October you will find the town

A classical doorway at Ehrenbreitstein, which became rich by dominating the river traffic where the Moselle meets the Rhine.

almost literally immersed in its annual wine festival.

At this point the Rhine makes a great loop and you find yourself driving west to Osterspai round the curve of the meander. Schloss Liebeneck on your left scarcely qualifies as a castle. Built as a hunting-lodge and summer holiday home around 1700, the *Schloss* is resolutely baroque despite its traditional round tower, a feature of every early medieval fortress.

Continue round the sweeping bend in the river to the half-timbered village of Filsen with its pretty seventeenth-century town hall. About 18 kilometres from Schloss Marksburg the two ruined castles of Kamp-Bornhofen are mute witnesses to the feuds which often split ambitious families in the Middle Ages. Known as the hostile brothers, they were built by two members of a lordly family thrown against each other out of love for the same woman. Heinrich and Konradin were the sons of the lord of Schloss Liebenstein. They both loved his adopted orphan, the exquisite Hildegarde. Whereas Heinrich kept his own counsel, Konradin declared his love and then went on a crusade. At last Heinrich too revealed his passion for Hildegarde. When Konradin returned from the Holy Land with a Greek bride, he moved into the second *Schloss*, Sterrenberg, built by his now deceased father. In a rage, Heinrich challenged Konradin to a duel. As they began to fight, Konradin's spurned bride Hildegarde interposed her lovely body between them to prevent one of the brothers killing the other. Then, refusing Heinrich's hand, she entered a nunnery. Heinrich followed suit and went into a monastery. The story ends when both he and she die on the same day.

Another pair of castles, united in friendship rather than hatred, lie a little further on. Burg Maus looms over the wine village of Wellmich, a few kilometres from its sister fortress at St Goarshausen, Burg Katz, which was built for Count Johann III von Katzenellenbogen in 1371. Just east along the B274 is the fourteenth-century Burg Reichenberg. And now we are only 4 kilometres from the most romantic stretch of the river, where the celebrated rock known as the Lorelei rises from the turbulent water. Of the many versions of the legend surrounding this place, none is better than Heinrich Heine's lovely lyric written in 1824 and set to haunting music by Friedrich Silchers in 1838. Aged 26, the poet had just been rejected by his cousin Amalia and was suffering the pangs of unrequited love. He was then spurned by her sister Therese. Heine's heartbreak was poured into his Lorelei, exquisite verse lamenting the misery of impotent passion, and the first German poem I ever committed to memory.

The legend concerns the water nymph Lore, who would sit on the top of the rock, luring men to their deaths. Her plaintive songs would so bewitch those sailing down the river that they would forget the dangerous rocks and reefs. Their boats would be wrecked and they themselves drowned. A mighty castle nearby was the home of Count Bruno and his son Hermann. Learning of Lore, Hermann felt himself inexorably drawn into hopeless love for a nymph he had yet to see. Bewitched, he would wander in the woods in the evening, singing of his enchantment. On one fateful day he saw Lore's exquisite form half-hidden in a cloud at the peak of the Lorelei rock. She was beckoning him and calling his name. Hermann sank to the ground unconscious and awoke in a trance. Count Bruno was deeply troubled by his son's state and sought to distract him by enlisting him as a soldier. The day before the lovesick youth was to leave for the army, Hermann decided to visit the Lorelei rock for the last time, taking a squire with him. They sailed downstream between the high banks of the Rhine,

Kamp-Bornhofen is dominated by Burg Sterrenberg and Burg Liebenstein, rival medieval castles which were occupied by two brothers who grew to hate each other in the fourteenth century.

Left **Burg Katz looms over the river above St Goar and St Goarshausen. One of the most romantic of the Rhine castles, it was built in the late fourteenth century by Count Johann III von Katzenellenbogen, hence its nickname. The counts of Katzenellenbogen also built Burg Reichenberg (***above***), now a powerful ruin.**

until the squire was filled with a sudden anxiety and begged to be put ashore. Hermann refused to land, and instead sang to Lore, vowing that he would willingly die for the nymph. Lore appeared on the flame-clad rock and beckoned to the waves. As Hermann's boat was overwhelmed, his squire was flung ashore. Hermann himself sank beneath the waters.

Mark Twain made a translation of Heine's poem which completely captures the spirit of the original and has the added virtue of also matching Friedrich Silchers's music:

I cannot divine what this meaneth,
This haunting nameless pain:
A tale of bygone ages
Keeps brooding through my brain:

The faint air cools in the gloaming,
And peaceful flows the Rhine,
The thirsty summits are drinking
The sunset's flooding wine;

The loveliest maiden is sitting
High-throned in yon blue air,
Her golden jewels are shining,
She combs her golden hair;

She combs with a comb that is golden,
And sings a weird refrain
That steeps in a deadly enchantment
The listener's ravished brain:

The doomed in his drifting shallop,
Is tranced with the sad sweet tone,
He sees not the yawning breakers,
He sees but the maid alone:

The pitiless billows engulf him! –
So perish sailor and bark;
And this with her baleful singing,
Is the Lorelei's gruesome work.

Another evocative sight in this part of the Rhine valley is the view of Burg Gutenfels from the road outside Kaub. Restored in the nineteenth century, this fearsome castle was originally built 700 years ago to dominate the river and collect tolls from those who sailed by. During the Thirty Years' War it became the headquarters of the Swedish King Gustavus Adolphus, and subsequent military commanders unerringly spotted the strategic importance of this site. Napoleon's bold General Blücher, for example, crossed the Rhine here on the first day of 1814. Today Kaub is noteworthy not so much for its former bristling warlike self as for its sweet twelfth-century church, the wine festival it hosts every September and the patrician houses in its market square. And rising serenely in the middle of the river is the so-called 'stone ship', the toll station on the island of Pfalzgrafenstein (see p.136).

Further south along the B42 you reach Lorch am Rhein, still ringed by the remains of medieval town walls. The eleventh-century Burg Nollich broods over the place and there is also a thirteenth-century church dedicated to St Martin which has a superb high altar created some 200 years later. Lorch is better known for its red wines, a foretaste of those to come further south. Drive on through the spa of Assmannshausen, take a glass of red wine there, and after another 5 kilometres or so the road reaches magical, fortified Rüdesheim.

The fact that Rüdesheim is invariably packed with visitors who have come here to sample the wine is thought by some to be a reason for not lingering here. This is nonsense. Rüdesheim's Thrush Alley (Drosselgasse), although perhaps crowded with pedestrians, is also lined with exquisite seventeenth- and eighteenth-century houses and inns. And the market square is

St Goarshausen lies under the protection of Burg Katz.

179

Above **This elaborate porch belongs to a house in Lorch built in the mid sixteenth century for the imperial field marshal Johann Hilchen.**

Right **The proud vines of Rüdesheim, the most famous in the Rhine valley.**

dominated by the early fifteenth-century church of St James. I am less fond of the ridiculously pretentious *Germania* which the sculptor J. Schilling shamelessly created in 1883 to glorify the short-lived German empire. These memorials to human *hubris* which are never regarded with affection seem to me monstrously pathetic. Symbolizing an utterly unacceptable, aggressive nationalism, arrogant *Germania* is my favourite example of mankind's sad tendency to identify with unthinking brutality while regarding this sentiment as something noble. At least you do not have to exhaust yourself climbing up to the monument – a cable-car takes you all the way. But the main reason for coming to Rüdesheim is to drink the Rieslings of the Rheingau, devastatingly potent fruit liqueurs and a sparkling German Sekt. The word 'Rüdesheimer' decorating a wine label is a guarantee of fragrance and quality. And every time I have visited Rüdesheim I have come upon a uniformed brass band playing in its streets.

Four kilometres to the east is the ancient town of Geisenheim, where no one should miss the gothic church with a baroque high altar known as the cathedral of the Rheingau. Geisenheim is also noteworthy as the place where the Thirty Years' War was finally brought to an end in 1648. You can still see Schloss Shönborn where the treaty was negotiated, as well as a lime tree that was planted 300 years before the war began. Those with more gastronomic interests might prefer to seek out the Hesse institute of wine culture. It is also worth driving 3 kilometres to the north to find the medieval monastery church of Marienthal, set in the midst of green forests. Then continue to Schloss Johannisberg, built on the site of an abandoned Benedictine abbey in the early eighteenth century by the architect Johannes Dient-

Vineyards rise above the Hotel Lindenwirt at Rüdesheim.

As this delightful carving shows, even the birds appreciate the quality of the grapes from Rüdesheim.

zenhofer and now reputed for the lovely wines that bear its name.

The road to Mittelheim from here passes through Winkel where you can see the oldest dwelling in the whole of Germany, the Graues Haus, said to have been built around 800. I do not believe this is true. The house is certainly ancient, but no older, I think, than the eleventh century. At Mittelheim the parish church dedicated to St Giles is the oldest in the Rheingau and seems unchanged since it was built in 1138. St Giles is the patron saint of cleaners and is said to help those tracing lost property. Another survival is to be seen at the little wine town of Oestrich to the east, where a wooden crane built in 1652 for use in the wine trade overhangs the Rhine. The half-timbered houses of this

Left Gay dormer windows and tiles in Hallgarten, north of Winkel.

Above An exquisite detail from a medieval house in Hattenheim, which also boasts a lovely parish church dedicated to Our Lady in her Assumption.

delightful place nestle beneath the heights of the Johannisberg.

Hattenheim, 3 kilometres east of Oestrich, has both a partly ruined *Schloss*, dating from the early fifteenth century, and a second castle with an elegant eighteenth-century façade by the riverside. Look for the signs from here directing you to the great Cistercian abbey of Kloster Eberbach. A monastery was first founded in this sheltered remote valley in 1116 and was raised to the status of an abbey 15 years later by St Bernard of Clairvaux. The abbey church is as plain as the sternest Cistercian would desire, but the monks who lived and prayed here dedicated themselves to growing grapes as well as to the worship of God. They deserve a prayer of thanks from every twentieth-century wine-bibber, for from the twelfth century onwards the fine grapes they cultivated in the nearby vineyards immeasurably enhanced the quality of the wine from this region. Soon Kloster Eberbach was producing more wine than any other single centre in Germany. Take a day to visit this evocative place and stroll slowly through its thirteenth-century refectory, its mid fourteenth-century chapter-house and the peaceful cloisters. Above all view the wine cellar, with its old wine-presses and a collection of venerable wine glasses. Then buy a bottle or two to take away with you.

This area known as the Rheingau lying north of the great curve of the Rhine has been renowned for its wine for centuries, judged by many to be the finest in all Germany. The country around Kloster Eberbach is dotted with charming wine villages, each surrounded by a trelliswork of vineyards crossing the hills where

Contrasting half-timbered houses at Eltville, the oldest town in the Rheingau, with a splendid promenade along the river.

Another glimpse of half-timbered Eltville, where the keep alone remains from the *Schloss* of the electors of Mainz.

plants are tied in traditional patterns, sometimes heart-shaped, sometimes spread out along the trellises like little trees. Kiedrich is a gothic town with a lovely fifteenth-century church dedicated to St Valentine. The *Schloss* dominating Eltville was the favourite home of the electors of Mainz, who perhaps liked to visit the late medieval church with its beautiful Madonna. This village has some fame today as a centre for the sparkling wines of the region. I had neglected them till I reached this spot and discovered that you can visit huge wine cellars here and watch the delicate process of creating a fragrant masterpiece that tickles the tongue and puts a lingering sparkle into the heart.

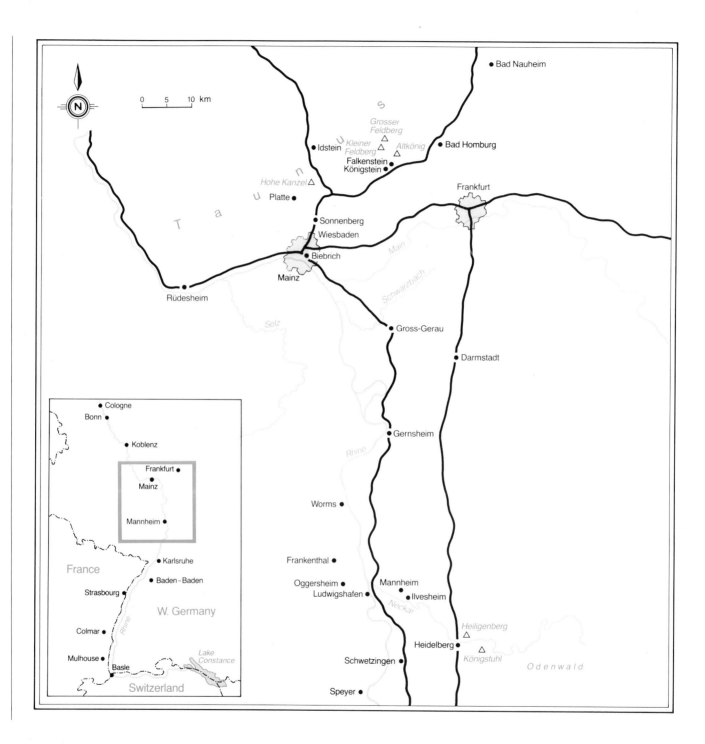

6
Elegant Spas and Duelling Students

Wiesbaden – Idstein – Königstein – Bad Homburg –
Gross-Gerau – Gernsheim – Worms –
Frankenthal – Ludwigshafen – Mannheim –
Heidelberg – Speyer

Stretching along the lower reaches of the River Main is the splendid mountain range known as the Taunus, richly clad in inky-black forests, slit with patches of cultivated land and clearings in the valleys and gashed with the occasional slate quarry. As the Taunus slopes towards the Rhine, the mountain pinewoods gradually start giving way to vineyards and orchards and a rustling multitude of chestnut trees. The westernmost point of the Taunus is the wine village of Rüdesheim. To the east it reaches almost as far as Bad Nauheim, some 70 kilometres as the crow flies. Craggy peaks range its course. The highest form a cluster north of Königstein, where the 825-metre Kleiner Feldberg is just topped by the Grosser Feldberg, 54 metres higher. Their companion the Altkönig, 'old king', rises a very close third at 798 metres. Over to the west is the intriguingly named Hohe Kanzel, the 'high pulpit', in fact less than 600 metres high. Then comes the lowly Trompeter, but 540 metres high. Originally volcanic, this walkers' paradise is studded with spa towns based on the mineral-rich springs.

Wiesbaden is the noblest spa of the whole region, sandwiched between the Taunus and the Rhine and sheltered by the mountains from cold winds from the north. There are no fewer than 27 thermal springs here, visited and drunk since Roman times for their healing properties. The most powerful source of these curative waters is the Kochbrunnen, whose 15 springs pour out 500,000 litres a day at an incredible maximum temperature of 67.5° Centigrade. As the Roman natural historian Pliny observed, 'the waters of this city across the Rhine are warm'.

Traces of the Roman baths' 'complex' have been found close to the remains of temples to the pagan gods Mithras and Jupiter. These Romans called Wiesbaden *Aquae Mattiacorum* after the Celtic tribe, the Mattiaci, whose territory they were occupying. Wiesbaden is to my mind a sweeter name, for it means 'springs in the meadow'. The present-day bathing establishments and the Trinkhalle are all clustered together at the north end of the delightfully flowery Wilhelmstrasse. The late nineteenth-century Trinkhalle, designed, as its name implies, for drinking the water rather than bathing in it, is built around a charming garden enclosed on three sides by colonnades. The Kurhaus itself, fronted by a lake from which water drips tentatively from heavy fountains, is truly impressive, as is the park in which it stands. Friedrich von Thiersch designed it in 1905, incorporating the old early nineteenth-century Kursaal which had become too small to cater for the visitors who now flocked annually to Wiesbaden. Like most buildings in Germany's spas dedicated to pandering to those suffering from over-indulgence in the good things of life, it is severely classical, with a massive Ionic portico beckoning the visitor. By contrast, the interior is richly decorated in pink and grey marble.

The fact that the Kurhaus houses a couple of concert halls (one of them the old Kursaal, the other a huge cavern supported by 28 Corinthian columns) indicates that the pursuit of health has never been the sole reason for these German spas. As the inevitable casino flanking von Thiersch's Kurhaus suggests, gambling has always been of equal importance. Dostoevsky and Turgenev played baccarat and roulette here, perhaps regaling themselves in one of the numerous bars which encourage visitors to the spa to forget that they are here for the good of their health. What he saw inspired Dostoevsky to write his novel *The Gambler*. South-west of the Kurhaus and spa stand the elegant baths of

Kaiser Friedrich, built in the second decade of this century, together with a clinic devoted to the estimable and (I think) hopeless aim of finding a cure for rheumatism. Nagel's *Encyclopedia Guide to Germany* adds that these springs also cure 'locomotor ataxia, slipped discs, traumas and catarrh'. How miraculous this would be if it were true!

What I find strange is the absence of ancient buildings in this elegant, fashionable and attractive city. Apart from its old town hall, Wiesbaden is almost entirely a creation of the nineteenth and early twentieth centuries. Fascinatingly, Goethe visited the city in 1814 and spotted precisely what was happening. The city architect, Johann Christian Zais, had just finished building a new Kursaal and Goethe approved of it. 'Those interested in architecture will find pleasure and a good style in the great Kursaal, as well as in the newly laid-out streets,' he reported. 'The large rooms which are being built in the new houses', he continued, 'awaken the hope that many a project, silently cherished, may be carried out here, and that a town which is so much visited and daily increasing in size may be rendered more important still by art collections and scientific institutions.'

The city's main street, the Wilhelmstrasse, is named after Wilhelm von Nassau who decreed that it should be traced out in 1812. Seven years later it led to the new palace of the dukes of Nassau, still to be seen at the corner of Wilhelmstrasse and Friedrichstrasse. Packed with banks, shops, boutiques and hotels, Wilhelm-strasse is the heart of the spa. William Wordsworth, coming here in 1820, was another visitor who approved of what he saw. The people no longer wear the bourgeois and peasant costumes he remarked on, but I entirely agree with his judgment that the town is

A fountain in the Kurhaus gardens, Wiesbaden, where even those not attracted to the spa baths can find peace.

'rather a handsome mixture of German stateliness and watering-place finery'.

Goethe would have relished the civic museum, housed in a massive early twentieth-century building by Theodor Fischer and packed with Roman and palaeolithic finds, medieval treasures and works by a whole galaxy of twentieth-century painters. These include 21 paintings by Wiesbaden's own Expressionist, the Russian-born Alexej von Jawlensky, who died here in 1941. The next time I am in the city I must find out whether the museum has preserved a celebrated collection of butterflies from the Taunus mountains which Goethe managed to have transferred here from Frankfurt. As was his unfortunate habit almost everywhere he went, Goethe fell in love at Wiesbaden. The hapless victim this time was Marianne von Willemar, who it seems gained little from the relationship. Posterity gained another lovely cycle of love poems.

The oldest surviving building in Wiesbaden is the town hall in Marktstrasse, built in 1610. There is also a new town hall, a splendid renaissance building of 1887, designed by the Munich architect Georg von Hauberrisser. The citizens of Wiesbaden must love it, for after their new town hall was virtually destroyed in World War II they meticulously restored it. Overlooking the market square is the city's impressive Protestant church, raised over ten years from 1852. Built of polished bricks, its five great towers shadow the stalls below, the chief tower rising some 100 metres. In case you think you have gone much further back in history when you reach the 'Roman gate', the truth is that it was built in 1902.

Not many early twentieth-century architects have managed to create satisfying monumental buildings, but Wiesbaden's congress hall (the Rhein-Main-Halle) is just such a building, designed by Theodor Fischer in 1912 and now housing the city museum. Naturally enough, since we are in a Roman city, the displays include the arms, jewels, gravestones and other remains of this great civilization. Here too are palaeolithic tombs and relics of the Frankish Merovingian Kingdom, at its height in the mid sixth century.

But the tone of the whole city is set by the Kurhausplatz with its fountains and colonnades. On one side rises von Thiersch's Kurhaus. On another stands the elegant Brunnenkolonnade, built in 1825. Opposite, porticoes shelter shops and fashionable stores, as well as the entrance to the civic theatre. Wiesbaden is culturally international. Distinguished foreign companies arrive here every May to perform music, ballet and drama in the theatre and in the concert halls of the Kurhaus and Brunnenkolonnade. I must confess that I have never dug deep enough in my pocket to attend one of these performances, but I have gained enormous pleasure from the open-air concerts held in the park north of the Kurhaus in summer.

The most touching building in the whole city stands on the forested Neroberg, which you can ascend by a steep twisting path or by the relative comfort of a rack-and-pinion railway. Five gilded onion domes, each topped by a Russian double cross, crown a Byzantine-style Russian Orthodox church, built to house the corpse of Elisabeth Michaïlovna, daughter of Duke Michael of Russia. This tragic Russian duchess, the first wife of Count Adolf von Nassau, died in 1855 only one year after the couple had married. The architect of her tomb was a German named Philipp Hofmann, but the court artist of St Petersburg was employed to paint the holy iconostasis, or altar screen. In the marble interior Countess Elisabeth lies in a marble sarcophagus surrounded by frescoes of the twelve apostles and the four theological virtues (faith, hope, charity and eternal life). For some extraordinary reason this Russian Orthodox mausoleum is always called the 'Greek church'.

After visiting the Russian Orthodox church on the Neroberg, you could indulge yourself in the open-air swimming-pool on its slopes. Then drive south

through the horse chestnuts along the Rheingaustrasse to the suburb of Biebrich on the Rhine, an important crossing-point even in the late ninth century when sailors made a profitable living by ferrying people across the river. Today this strategic spot is dominated by the magnificent mid eighteenth-century baroque palace of the counts of Nassau, now the headquarters of a German film company. Commercial considerations have in no way detracted from the beauty of the place. Schloss Biebrich is a study in white and yellow, its entrancing double staircase climbing gracefully to a round central hall, its long matching wings as elegant as they are imposing. The extensive park (50 hectares set out in the naturalistic, so-called 'English' style by Friedrich Ludwig von Sckell in 1811) is graced by another *Schloss*, the pseudo-medieval Moosburg which was built in 1810. If all this seems falsely romantic, it was Biebrich that inspired Richard Wagner while he was writing his *Mastersingers of Nuremberg*.

A genuine medieval ruin lies north-east of Wiesbaden, reached along the pretty Rambach valley. The suburb of Sonnenberg is dominated by the ruins of a feudal castle built in the early thirteenth century by the counts of Nassau. The French demolished most of it in 1689, but the keep still stands and you can climb its 116 steps for a panoramic view of the surrounding countryside.

West across country from here the counts' hunting *Schloss* stands 500 metres high in the forest above the little town of Platte. The N275 leads you on to the sheltered, half-timbered town of Idstein, dominated for four centuries by the lords of Nassau-Idstein who now lie crowded together in the fifteenth-century church at the foot of the peak which they crowned with a *Schloss* in 1634. The ceremonial Burg gate was

One of the many Gutenberg statues dotting the Rhine valley, this one showing him unusually at ease, since he was continually persecuted by those to whom he owed money.

built in 1497 to commemorate a visit by the Emperor Maximilian I. It stands next to the witches' tower, all that remains of an eleventh-century feudal castle.

Königstein is another romantic little town in the Taunus mountains north of Wiesbaden, now a popular summer resort. The attractions here include the ruins of castle Königstein and a picturesque mid nineteenth-century grand-ducal *Schloss*. A short distance away is the village of Falkenstein, clustered around the eleventh-century ruins of Schloss Falkenstein. You are now only a few kilometres from the Grosser Feldberg, the highest peak of the Taunus mountains, with a welcome restaurant right at the top. To the east, a three-hour hike away, lies the spa of Bad Homburg, with a lovely park, a late seventeenth-century *Schloss*

The statue of the dramatist Friedrich Schiller fronting the elegant civic theatre of Wiesbaden.

and the inevitable elegant baths, casino, tennis courts and golf courses. From here you can take the motorway back to Wiesbaden.

Leave the city by driving south-east to Gross-Gerau and then south along the luscious Rhine valley. At the little port of Gernsheim on the way there is a statue erected to Gutenberg's assistant Schöffer. A few kilometres further on a bridge over the Rhine leads to the ancient city of Worms, set some 400 metres above the river with vineyards stretching away in all directions. You would never guess how old Worms was, wandering the streets, for 65 per cent of the city was destroyed towards the end of World War II. One hint that the place may be older than it seems is the huge Jewish cemetery, the largest and earliest in Europe, on the Andreas Ring. It dates from the eleventh century, when one-third of the population of Worms was Jewish. The synagogue itself is in Judengasse, near the spot where a ritual Jewish women's bathhouse or *Mikwe* was discovered in 1900, dating from 1186. Until World War II the synagogue was as old as the cemetery and was one of the few buildings to have survived the pillage and fire of 1689. Then, on the infamous *Kristallnacht* of 9 November 1938, the Nazis destroyed it. In 1961 a new building rose from the ashes. The whole Jewish quarter of Worms has been carefully reconstructed and is now a protected area.

Two outstanding romanesque churches have also survived from the ancient city. The earlier, the church of St Paul, was finished in 1016. The cathedral, with its four magnificent towers and two domes, was begun about a hundred years later. Its west end was finished by 1181. I never fail to be impressed by this great church, 158 metres long and rising 40 metres to the dome which soars above the crossing. Since it also boasts a glittering baroque high altar by Balthasar Neumann, superb eighteenth-century choir-stalls by an unknown genius and thirteenth-century frescoes, Worms cathedral should not be missed. Watch out for the twelfth-century sculpture of Jesus sitting in judgment (the *Thronender Christus*) just inside the south portal. And notice the two apses, one at either end of the church, an oddity of German romanesque architecture. The beautifully simple east end was reserved for the priests and acolytes, for great churchmen, and for the celebration of the holy office. The west apse, designed for the Holy Roman Emperor and the great civic dignitaries of the city, is more complex but still beautiful. The Holy Roman Emperor often sat here, for more than a hundred imperial Diets were held at Worms. I like to sit here too, quietly admiring the twelve segments of the great rose window.

The name of the great Protestant reformer Martin Luther is inseparable from that of Worms. This one-time Augustinian monk became professor of theology at Wittenberg university in 1511. Several visits to Rome convinced him of the corruption of the papacy, which he proceeded to attack in his writings and teachings. The pope excommunicated him and Luther was then summoned to the celebrated Diet of Worms held in 1521, where his works were condemned. Many thought Luther would have been too afraid to come, or, if he came, that he would recant of his attacks on the Pope. Martin Luther was not only brave but also robustly witty. 'This shall be my recantation,' he wrote to a friend after the emperor's invitation to come to Worms had arrived. 'At Worms I shall say, "Previously I asserted that the pope is the vicar of Christ. I recant. Now I say that the pope is the adversary of Christ and the apostle of the Devil." '

At Worms Luther was faced by the Emperor Charles V, six electors and a huge assembly of notables. He ended his self-defence with the famous words, 'Here I stand. I can do no other. So help me God.' Neither his courage nor his theological arguments allowed him to escape censure. The Edict of Worms, signed by Emperor Charles V, declared 'He has sullied marriage, disparaged confession and denied the body and blood

Hagen casts the Nibelung treasure into the Rhine at Worms, precariously balanced in a fragile boat.

of our Lord.' So far one might conclude that these godly men were simply disagreeing about theology. But mere theological disagreement was not enough in this strife-torn era. The Edict of Worms continues:

'This devil in the habit of a monk has brought together ancient errors in one stinking puddle and has invented new ones. He denies the power of the keys and encourages the laity to wash their hands in the blood of the clergy. His teaching makes for rebellion, division, war, murder, robbery, arson and the collapse of Christendom. He lives the life of a beast.'

It concluded with the vain decree that: 'His books are to be eradicated from the memory of man.'

It was all to no avail. Today a mighty bronze monument to the great reformer, designed by Ernest Rietschel in 1868, forms the centrepiece of the Lutherplatz. At Luther's feet stand sculpted figures of lesser but still renowned reformers – John Wycliffe, Jan Huss, Philip Melanchthon and Girolamo Savonarola – as well as of the enlightened princelings who protected them. Here too are represented three other great cities: Augsburg in a pose of repentance; Magdeburg, mourning; and Speyer, protesting. The 24 coats of arms on this complex nineteenth-century monument to Protestantism are those of the first two dozen cities to embrace the Reformation.

Legends as well as centuries of history pervade this city. One is about the vineyards rising to either side of the celebrated cruciform fifteenth-century church of Our Lady. The wine produced here is known as Our Lady's milk, or Liebfraumilch. The story concerns an old nobleman who lived nearby long ago. Pious and generous, he had only one fault: he drank more wine than was good for him. The devil, disliking the old man's piety, determined to use this weakness to trap him. Disguising himself as a wandering musician, the evil one came to the nobleman's household and began to speak of a wondrous wine which he had drunk in the south, so entrancing the noble drinker that he eventually promised anything in return for some of this nectar. Satan revealed himself, claimed the man's soul and planted a new vineyard on his lands. When the wine was harvested it did indeed prove magical. Enraptured, the old nobleman baptised it 'the milk of Our Lady', to the devil's deep anger. The Blessed Virgin, on the other hand, was extremely pleased, and when Satan came to claim the old man's soul, she sent angels to drive him away. The nobleman repented of his folly in bartering with the devil, and built a chapel in the midst of his vineyards, dedicated to the Virgin Mary, said to be the forerunner of the present fine church with its lovely carved choir-stalls.

Equally renowned is the saga of the Nibelungs, based on a medieval epic poem in which the hero Siegfried kills the Nibelungs and seizes their treasure –

and immortalized in Wagner's operatic cycle *The Ring of Nibelung*. On the Nibelung bridge spanning the Rhine a statue of Siegfried's enemy Hagen is depicted casting the treasure into the river. By the time the saga reaches this point, Siegfried has already been treacherously slain by Hagen. Although bathing in the blood of the dragon that guarded the treasure in a cave in the Siebengebirge to the north (see p.167) had made Siegfried virtually invulnerable, a linden leaf had fallen between his shoulders as he bathed. Feigning a desire to protect Siegfried should this one vulnerable spot ever be exposed, Hagen induced Siegfried's wife Kriemhild to tell him precisely where the leaf had fallen. Then, when Siegfried was drinking from a stream, he plunged the hero's own spear between his shoulders and killed him.

Kriemhild now found herself the guardian of the Nibelung treasure, which she gave away to princes and knights round about to secure their support. Hagen became anxious she would soon have made so many allies as to be able to rise up against him, so he seized the treasure and threw it into the Rhine. His statue at Worms depicts him standing in a ridiculously inadequate boat. Why doesn't it overturn?

The B9 now runs along the left bank of the Rhine, passes under the motorway from Mannheim and 2 kilometres later reaches the sizeable industrial town of Frankenthal. When the Spaniards expelled Protestants from their part of the Netherlands in the seventeenth century, many took refuge here. As usual, they brought considerable entrepreneurial skills, and in the eighteenth century developed a profitable porcelain industry. The two ornate eighteenth-century town gates both derive from this period. The ruins of a twelfth- and thirteenth-century romanesque monastery in a park behind the classical Catholic church are relics of the medieval town.

Father Rhine.

Ten kilometres later you reach the suburb of Ludwigshafen known as Oggersheim. Here is an unexpected treat. In 1729 the crown prince of the house of Palatinate-Sulzbach built a pretty chapel, dedicated to the Assumption of the Blessed Virgin Mary, which soon became a celebrated place of pilgrimage. So many crowded to pray here that in the 1770s the architect Peter Anton Verschaffelt rebuilt the church. The building is intriguing for several reasons. It is one of Verschaffelt's very few ecclesiastical buildings and what he created is an architectural oddity, a Roman baroque church on the banks of the Rhine. Thirdly, it is known particularly for the model behind its high altar of the Holy House of Loreto – that remarkable building said to have been commissioned by the Empress Helena, mother of the Emperor Constantine, to mark the Virgin Mary's birthplace in Nazareth and miraculously transported by angels to Ancona and then Loreto in Italy. Schillerstrasse is another eponymous feature of Oggersheim, named after the poet and dramatist Friedrich Schiller who spent some months in 1782 living at no. 6, writing his *Kabale und Liebe* ('Intrigue and Love').

For a city on the Rhine Ludwigshafen itself comes as a complete surprise, for it hardly existed 200 years ago. Ludwigshafen is called after King Ludwig I of Bavaria, who founded it in 1843 on the site of an early seventeenth-century fortification known as the Rheinschanze. Now the centre of the German chemical industry, its authorities have made up for the lack of ancient buildings by constructing a massive sports centre capable of holding 85,000 spectators, and by creating a lovely park (the Ebertpark) as well as garden promenades along the river bank.

Mannheim on the other side of the Rhine is a complete contrast, although it too is a city of lovely parks and gardens, with the Stephanienpromenade equalling the attractions on the opposite bank. But there is no escaping the fact that Mannheim is 250 years older than its sister city. The little fishing village that had existed here from the mid eighth century was transformed in 1606, when the architects of the Elector Friedrich IV arrived to lay out a remarkable new town to a grid pattern that survives to this day. No houses and few streets were named, letters and numbers identifying most of the rectangular blocks, 136 of which are still known in this way. Elector Friedrich's architects included some of the most distinguished Italians of his day as well as the Dutchman Bartel Janson, who conceived the plan of setting streets out like a chess board, rigidly at right-angles to each other. But credit for this odd, strange city must ultimately be given to the elector. No modern device, however bizarre, was unacceptable to this innovative man. In Paradeplatz, for instance, he commissioned Gabriel Grupello to design a quaint bronze fountain in the form of a pyramid. Later in the seventeenth century the French besieged and partly demolished Mannheim, but Elector Johann Wilhelm set about rebuilding it along his predecessor's lines.

The *Schloss* at Mannheim must be the most sumptuous university in Germany, a splendid white and pink baroque palace built between 1720 and 1760, its façade stretching for some 190 metres. Its great staircase chamber was decorated by C. D. Asam, and, though destroyed by the bombs of World War II, it has been meticulously restored using the evidence of photographs. Asam also decorated the *Schloss* church, which was demolished during an air raid and has been extremely well rebuilt. This building is delightfully surrounded by a 38-hectare garden, running for a thousand or so metres along the Rhine. Opposite the *Schloss* stands the late eighteenth-century Palais Bretzenheim, on block A2 according to the elector's numbering. After World War II only its façade and staircase were faithfully restored and the building now houses a bank.

To the north-west of the magnificent university *Schloss*, block A5 contains the Jesuit church, begun in

1731, eleven years after the Elector Palatine had moved his capital here from Heidelberg. He had become a Catholic and felt ill at ease in the Protestant city. Again, its architect was no German but the Italian Alessandro Galli-Bibbiena of Bologna. Its baroque pulpit was a casualty of World War II, but another one was brought from a Heidelberg church. Next door is the city's eighteenth-century observatory.

Just as Mannheim has skilfully transformed the electoral *Schloss* into its university, so today the elector's *Zeughaus* (or arsenal), built on block C5 in 1779, is a museum devoted to the art and history of the city. The displays include a model of the world's first bicycle, invented at Mannheim in 1817, as well as some fantastic baroque sculptures.

Apart from the glories of its gardens, one of the attractions of Mannheim in the spring is the traditional May market, first held some three centuries ago. Festive crowds consume a festival cake called *Mannemer Dreck*. And they drink. At Mannheim Goethe and a couple of friends, including Count Leopold Stolberg, once behaved abominably as a result of drinking too much of the town's excellent wine. They occupied what Goethe himself described as 'pleasant chambers in a respectable hotel'. At their first dinner there all went well until the dessert. They had not spared the wine, and Count Leopold challenged his two companions to drink the health of his lady. This, according to Goethe's own account, was done noisily enough. When the glasses were drained, Leopold cried out, 'Now, out of vessels thus consecrated, no more drinking can be allowed. A second toast would be a blasphemy. Let us annihilate these goblets.' With these words he dashed his glass against the wall behind

Pink sandstone flanks the market square of Mannheim, a small fishing village until it was transformed into the capital of the electorate in the seventeenth century.

him, and his two companions followed suit. What the landlord of this respectable hotel thought, Goethe does not record.

During Mannheim's May market similar feasting in the market square takes place in the shadow of a splendid parish church, built between 1701 and 1723. There are also modern buildings here – as in all these German cities which suffered so greatly during World War II. The theatre where Schiller's *Die Räuber*, *Kabale und Liebe* and *Fiesko* were first performed had to be rebuilt in 1955 to a design by Gerhard Weber. The Luisenpark, with its zoo and floating stage, is dominated by a television tower, 205 metres high, topped by one of those revolving restaurants where surely only the lunatic eat. Bafflingly, this baroque city has chosen as its emblem the water-tower which was constructed in Friedrichsplatz in 1888 and which is surrounded by delicious art nouveau buildings. It is, I concede, one of the most monumental water-towers imaginable.

You can drive speedily from Mannheim to Heidelberg along the motorway which closely follows the River Neckar. But it is better to take Bundestrasse 37 through Ilvesheim in order to see the former *Schloss* of the lords of Hundheim, built around 1700 by Johann Adam Breunig. You could also go by boat, although as the Neckar has now been tamed by canalization your journey is unlikely to be as memorable as William Wordsworth's. Travelling from Heidelberg downstream in a tiny vessel, he was so affected by the rapid over which his craft plunged that he composed a poem afterwards in the form of a prayer:

> Jesu! bless our slender Boat,
> By the current swept along;
> Loud its threatenings – let them not
> Drown the music of a song
> Breathed thy mercy to implore,
> Where these troubled waters roar.

Heidelberg itself is a lovely city picturesquely standing at the point where the Neckar descends from the hilly forests of the Odenwald into the Rhine plain. From everywhere in the city you can see the peak known as the Königstuhl, 568 metres high, which towers over Heidelberg to the east. There are spectacular views of the *Schloss* on the slopes of the mountain from the cable-car to the summit.

Heidelberg university is the oldest in Germany, founded by Rupert I and given its charter by Pope Urban VI in 1386. In the palaeontological institute you can see the Heidelberg jaw, a 400,000-year-old fossil belonging to the species generally known as *homo erectus*, but which the people here call *homo Heidelbergensis*. The university was long renowned for its fighting students, who puzzled Mary Shelley in 1820 for not dressing in a sober, scholarly fashion – that is to say exactly like most twentieth-century students. 'They wear whatever wild and coarse apparel pleases them – their hair long and disorderly – or rough as a water-dog – throats bare – or with a black collar – and often no appearance of a shirt,' she complained.

Mark Twain discovered them duelling, and has left us a splendid description of this now abandoned pursuit. Two bare-headed combatants entered the room, iron goggles protecting their eyes, their necks wound round with thick wrappings, their bodies stoutly covered from chin to ankle. As an additional precaution, a grey-haired surgeon was always in attendance, with lint, bandages and instruments.

Then the youths began to strike at each other, their swords wielded with tremendous force. 'Presently, in the midst of the sword-flashes, I saw a handful of hair skip into the air as if it had lain loose on the victim's

The courtyard of the *Schloss* at Heidelberg, an entrancing half-ruined castle which dominates the whole city.

head and a breath of wind had puffed it suddenly away,' recorded Mark Twain. The stewards cried halt. The surgeon inspected the wound – a crimson gash two or three inches long – and bound some lint over it. Then the duel recommenced. Swords were broken into fragments and replaced. The duellers were occasionally given a moment's rest, or earned one by wounding each other. Normally duels lasted 15 minutes, but this did not include the pauses. In consequence it was usually about half an hour before the students were judged too weary to fight on. 'They were led away, drenched from head to foot.' Mark Twain was told that this was a good fight, but could not count as a proper one partly because the actual duelling time did not quite amount to 15 minutes and partly because neither combatant was disabled by his wounds. The rules of the game demanded that the adversaries should do battle again as soon as they were recovered.

When not duelling, the students seemed to Mark Twain to spend most of their time swilling vast amounts of beer out of pint mugs. At beer-drinking competitions each competitor counted the number of pints he had consumed by putting a matchstick on the table for each one downed. The student who drank the most – frequently by vomiting to make more space in his stomach – was proclaimed king for the evening.

High above the town and the river rises Heidelberg's red sandstone *Schloss*, created over five centuries. The first time I was in Heidelberg I took the unwise advice of a guidebook and climbed up to the *Schloss* by the twisting Burgweg – romantic enough, but extremely steep. My own recommendation is to take the cable-car up and walk down.

The building was begun in the thirteenth century. The French devastated the *Schloss* in 1689 and lightning demolished more in 1764. The finest parts surviving today are the two renaissance wings known as the Otto-Heinrichsbau and the Friedrichsbau, the second distinctively decorated with statues of the kings of Germany and the ancestors of the prince-electors who built the *Schloss*. Although the charm of this place lies partly in the fact that it is a romantic ruin, I take delight in the architectural contrasts between the gothic and the renaissance wings of what remains intact. Ludwig V, for example, who died in 1544, built the gothic library. Scarcely a decade later his nephew Otto Heinrich, who ruled Heidelberg for only three years from 1556 to 1559 and built the superb wing named after him, had renounced the gothic in favour of the Italian renaissance style.

The mid eighteenth-century inhabitants of the *Schloss* must have had a thirst for wine which matched the beer-swilling capacity of the students of the town, for the huge wine cask coopered in 1751 and displayed in the Friedrichsbau is capable of holding a staggering 185,500 litres. The legend is that an Italian court jester named Perkeo used to guard and frequently drink the wine of the Heidelberg Tun, as the cask is known. His nickname derives from a boast he made when asked if he could drink every single drop of wine in the huge cask. '*Perché no?*', he replied, Italian for 'Why not?', and Perkeo he became. One day Perkeo accidentally drank water, caught a chill and died. The citizens of Heidelberg have dedicated a huge beer and wine house (in Hauptstrasse) in memory of this jesting toper.

When Mary Shelley visited the castle in the 1840s she unconsciously displayed her blend of supposed egalitarianism and patronizing condescension to the lower orders. She and her friends were shown round by a woman whom she described as 'without being pretty, very agreeable; with gentle, courteous, and yet vivacious manners: she spoke English with a very pretty accent, and her laugh was soft and joyous'.

A renaissance archway leads to the exquisite *Schloss* garden in Heidelberg, first laid out by the luckless 'winter king' Friedrich V in the early seventeenth century.

Mary Shelley continued with the observation, 'It is always pleasant to meet, among the uneducated classes, individuals with whom you have lost all sense of *caste* – who are instantly on a level with those deemed their superiors, from mere force of engaging manners, intelligence, and apparent kindness of heart.' By contrast I was shown round Heidelberg *Schloss* with (it seemed to me) around 20,000 other visitors by a grumpy fool.

Later the same day I wandered at peace again amidst the exotic trees of the *Schloss* garden, first laid out by the unfortunate Friedrich V, who reigned for just a year. Filled with grottoes, statues, caves and ponds, the garden was mostly recreated in the nineteenth century after much of it was ruined during the Thirty Years' War. From the garden you can gaze at a ruined wing which once housed Friedrich's bride, Elizabeth, the tragic winter queen, eldest daughter of James I of Great Britain and his consort Anne of Denmark. Titular Queen of Bohemia, an alluring Scotswoman ultimately destined for misery, her life was always fraught with danger and surrounded with poetry. The gunpowder plotters who intended to blow up the English parliament in 1605 planned to proclaim her queen had their scheme succeeded. Her beauty inspired poets and tempted the dauphin, as well as Philip III of Spain, the Prince of Orange and Gustavus Adolphus of Sweden. But the astute politicians who guided Protestant Britain decided that a politic match with the Protestant Friedrich V, Elector Palatine, was more suited to Britain's interests.

On 17 June 1613 Friedrich and Elizabeth ceremoniously entered Heidelberg. Apart from the burdens of childbearing (she had thirteen children altogether), for five years her life was one of ostentation and self-indulgence. Then in 1618 the Bohemians deposed their emperor and appointed Elizabeth's husband Friedrich in his place. The following year the couple entered Prague in great pomp for their coronation. Alas, the citizens disapproved of Elizabeth's levity and skittishness. Soon her husband was himself deposed and forced to take refuge first in Berlin and then in Holland, where the House of Orange granted his wife a pension. Elizabeth's father refused to give his daughter's unfortunate husband any real help, though he did grant her an annuity of some £12,000. Duke Christian of Brunswick, the Earl of Craven and numerous other swains were taken by Elizabeth's beauty, but everyone proved faithless when she asked for practical assistance to regain her throne. In 1632 her husband died in exile.

To make matters worse, the English parliament, at odds with James I's successor Charles, cancelled her annuity. Her Dutch pension was stopped in 1650. Her children deserted her, and her eldest son – the elector palatine – refused to allow her into his electorate. Even Charles II, who was kindly disposed to Elizabeth, tried to stop her eventual return to England. The luckless woman finally returned to her homeland in 1661, with less than a year to live.

Curiously enough, Heidelberg, where this queen dogged by religious disputes was at her happiest, had set out to be a centre of religious reconciliation in the sixteenth century. The Elector Friedrich III (who liked to be known as Friedrich the Pious), though himself a devout and committed Calvinist, deeply deplored the way Protestants were divided against each other. In an attempt to bring the warring factions together, he instructed the leading theologians of Heidelberg university to draw up a catechism that would be acceptable to every sect. The theologians dutifully drew up a document with which they hoped every Protestant would agree. It eschewed all polemics, concentrating on piety and good works. None of the belligerent Protestants paid the remotest attention to it.

The modern city owes its present beauty indirectly to the initiative of Friedrich and Elizabeth's second son, Karl Ludwig, who returned to Heidelberg when the Thirty Years' War was over and set about repairing

Mute halbardiers guarding the *Schloss* at Heidelberg.

the damage. When he died in 1685 with no sons to succeed him, his daughter's marriage to the French Duke of Orleans was used by the predatory Louis XIV of France to claim Heidelberg and the surrounding countryside as his own. French troops destroyed old Mannheim and drove on to sack Heidelberg. Two buildings alone survived intact: a renaissance inn known as the Haus zum Ritter, where you can still stay and eat; and the church of the Holy Spirit.

The double-storeyed oriel windows and the entrancing gable of the Haus zum Ritter were built by a Huguenot merchant in 1592. Eating in the Knight's Hall here is still surprisingly cheap, though as one of Heidelberg's major tourist attractions its food is obviously not the least expensive in the city, and its chefs seem to go in for international cuisine as well as the traditionally heavy Heidelberg dishes. Cheaper,

yet equally celebrated, is the student tavern on Karlsplatz known as Zum Roten Ochsen, which was built in 1703. Its long oak tables groan to huge *Schnitzeln*, washed down with gargantuan *Steins* of beer, while patrons begin to sing in less and less perfect harmony as the evening wears on.

The church of the Holy Ghost (or Heiliggeistkirche) is in the market square, opposite the early eighteenth-century town hall, and delightfully crowded by little shops nestling between its buttresses. Built in the early fifteenth century, it is the largest gothic church in this part of Germany. Protestants in Heidelberg have the irritating habit (if I may say so) of locking their churches, so it is often difficult to see inside this lovely building, with its medieval tomb of Ruprecht III of the Palatine, who died in 1410, and his wife Elizabeth of Hohenzollern, and the unique galleries on each side of the nave, built to house the famous Palatine library. The rich store of manuscripts and books was carried off as booty to Rome by the Imperial Field Marshal Tilly during the Thirty Years' War, but Pope Pius VI honourably gave back over 800 German manuscripts in 1816. Though basically gothic, the church boasts an imposing mansard roof added in 1689 and an eighteenth-century baroque dome.

I have never failed to get into the Jesuit church in Schulgasse. The Jesuits had been expelled from Heidelberg in 1648 at the end of the Thirty Years' War but Elector Johann Wilhelm brought them back fifty years later and this church dates from that time. I do not claim it as one of the greatest churches of the Palatinate; it simply seems to me a highly satisfying house of God, its marbled apse just that little more colourful and ornate than the rest of the building as befits the holy of holies. The architect, Johann Adam Breunig, who designed it in 1712, also built much else in the city after the vicious attacks of the French. The baroque sculptures which are such a feature of this lovely church are by Paul Egell, who was working in Mannheim while Breunig was rebuilding Heidelberg.

205

Among Breunig's other buildings for Heidelberg is the early baroque museum (Kurpfälzische Museum) which graces the Hauptstrasse. It houses a masterpiece by Tilman Riemenschneider, mayor of Würzburg, whose gothic carvings in limewood and stone are the greatest of all time. His dazzling altar of the twelve apostles for Windsheim church, created in 1509, was crassly covered in layers of paint over the centuries and not recognized as Riemenschneider's work until it was cleaned after World War II. No one should leave Heidelberg without seeing it.

Hauptstrasse is today pedestrianized, separated from the River Neckar by the narrow streets of the old town. Follow the narrow Steingasse from Heilig-geistkirche to see the river open out before you and to cross the graceful old bridge (or Alte Brücke) – a faithful replica of the one built by Prince Elector Karl Theodor in the mid eighteenth century that was destroyed by American bombs in World War II. (The Americans paid for the rebuilding.) A delightful stone gateway with two white pepperpot towers guards the entrance to the bridge.

There are fine views of Heidelberg from here, but undoubtedly the best prospect of the city is from the Philosopher's Way, a path that winds steeply up the Heiligenberg on the other bank of the river, past a monument to Otto von Bismarck and a late nineteenth-century watch-tower 375 metres high. To reach the ruined eleventh-century monastery of St Michael 440 metres above sea-level at the top takes me about 30 minutes. If you do not fancy the climb, take the bus from Bismarckplatz.

Then leave the hills behind and drive south-west for 11 kilometres into the Rhine plain to the small town of Schwetzingen. After the French invasions the prince-electors built themselves a stunning summer palace here, finishing it in 1715. Around 1750 they added a delightful rococo theatre which in itself makes a visit worthwhile. But my greatest surprise was to find the best preserved baroque garden I have ever visited, the

creation of the architect Nicolas de Pigage (who designed Schwetzingen's rococo theatre); the land-scape gardener Friedrich Ludwig von Sckell; and the court gardener himself, Johann Ludwig Petri. The garden is adorned with engaging classical temples, a bathhouse and finally a mosque, around which von Sckell set out a Turkish garden.

As you drive on west from Schwetzingen back to the Rhine the six towers of the great sandstone cathedral of Speyer appear ahead on the other side of the river. Once again the French wreaked havoc here in 1689, but the walls of this church, the noblest romanesque basilica in the whole of the Rhineland, were spared. Built in the first half of the eleventh century, it once cared for the mortal remains of eight German emperors. The rampaging troops of Louis XIV pulled them out of their tombs and scattered their ashes. As Victor Hugo put it, 'they violated families; they violated religion; they violated the dead, obliterating along with majesty the whole history of a great people and all that survived from a great empire.' Speyer cathedral was restored in the eighteenth century, but then suffered again at the hands of the French when members of the Revolutionary army despoiled it in 1794. The great basilica was restored a second time fifty years later. A new, yet more fastidious restoration was carried out after World War II. Contemplating its crypt, the largest in Germany, what impresses me most is not so much its size but the beauty of the ancient vaulting, accentuated by being fretted in red and white stone.

Apart from Speyer cathedral little else survived the sack of 1689, although you can see a fine thirteenth-century gateway if you walk along Maximilianstrasse from here. On the way you pass the church of the Holy

The white towers of the Brückentor at Heidelberg defending the old bridge over the Neckar.

Left A silent harpist in Wiesloch's market square, a peaceful town south of Heidelberg.

Above The mighty cathedral of Speyer, whose foundation stone was laid in 1030, has the largest romanesque crypt in Christendom and was the burial place of eight emperors.

Left The harmonious west front of Speyer cathedral.

Above A renaissance knight observes visitors entering the wine museum at Speyer.

Trinity, built in the first half of the eighteenth century. Do try to find a moment to go inside. You can tell this is a Protestant church, for the whole emphasis is on preaching and music, with a double gallery like the tiers of a theatre. Yet the followers of what was often a rather austere faith worship in an unforgettably exuberant baroque interior.

Looking at Speyer's modern buildings I find it difficult to believe its history stretches back over 2000 years and that there was a fortified Roman town here which Tacitus described. Even more intriguing is the fact that the cathedral was chosen as the setting for the first meeting of a future British monarch and his bride-to-be. The future monarch, the amorous Edward VII, came here in September 1861 to inspect Alexandra of Schleswig-Holstein-Sonderburg-Glucksburg. In a vain attempt to stop his son's unacceptable dalliances, his father determined that Edward (or Bertie as the royal family called him) should be married as soon as possible and by 1858 no fewer than seven young women were being considered for the unenviable position of wife to a royal philanderer. Fifth down the list came Alexandra, daughter of the Danish royal family. In spite of her relatively lowly position in the pecking order of preference, Alexandra's cause was enthusiastically promoted at the court of Queen Victoria by the profligate prince's eldest sister, Vicky, already the wife of the future Kaiser of Germany. 'I have never set eyes on a sweeter creature than Princess Alex,' she told Victoria; 'she is lovely. Her voice, her walk, carriage and manner are perfect, she is one of the most ladylike and aristocratic looking people I ever saw.' Alexandra's prospects were further advanced when Edward himself saw a photograph of the favourite of the seven prospective brides, Elizabeth of Wied, and promptly rejected her on the grounds of her looks and her unprepossessing physique.

Nowhere in Speyer is far from refreshment.

Not that either Edward or Alexandra were perfect beauties. Self-indulgence had swollen the prince, cruelly but accurately nicknamed 'Tum-Tum'. Sweet, simple Alexandra suffered a disfiguring scar on her neck. Since the Danes were at odds with Germany over who should own Schleswig-Holstein, German supporters spread the rumour that this scar was the result of scrofula. In consequence, it was suggested, Alexandra might be barren. For her part the young princess coped with her disfigurement by wearing her hair in ringlets to conceal it. Later she affected a choker that hid the scar and thus, as Queen of Great Britain, set a fashion followed by many women not at all disfigured.

So it was arranged that Tum-Tum and Alexandra would meet in Speyer cathedral. He was entranced. This gross prince, whose own mother found him 'sallow, dull, heavy, blasé', rightly felt himself unfit for such a delightful bride. 'I only feared that I was not worthy of her', he wrote. Tum-Tum never expressed a truer word. For a short time he found it convenient not to ask for her hand in marriage, since he had taken up with the actress Nelly Cliften. Queen Victoria persisted with the alliance, in the conviction that Alexandra would be 'so pretty to live with'. Bertie and Alexandra were formally betrothed a year after they had first set eyes on each other in Speyer cathedral. I find it ironic that the alliance between a charming slightly dim princess and a man who would betray her for the rest of his life should have been initiated in this lovely house of God.

In front of the cathedral is the *Domnapf*, a huge bowl which was set up in 1490. Whenever a new bishop was elected, he was required to fill the *Domnapf* with wine. The citizens then drank his health. I do not know who the present Bishop of Speyer is, but surely all visitors should drink his health here, perhaps buying a more than usually expensive bottle in one of the city supermarkets and then drinking it in the cathedral garden under the eyes of long-dead emperors.

Index